Active Parenting for Stepfamilies™

For Parents & Stepparents

Michael H. Popkin, PhD

Elizabeth Einstein, MA, LMFT

ACTIVE
PARENTING™
PUBLISHERS

To my stepmother of 40 years, Naomi Popkin

-Michael Popkin

❖

To my sons, Christopher and Jeffrey, and to all my stepchildren: Cynthia
and Lynn; Beverly, Brenda and Kurt. Together we've learned a family is
not necessarily the one into which we were born nor are its members
related by blood. Love is the common denominator.

-Elizabeth Einstein

ISBN 978-1-59723-201-2

Cover design by Gabrielle Tingley

Printed in Canada

Table of Contents

Contents

Contents

Acknowledgements

From Michael Popkin: *Active Parenting for Stepfamilies* is based on the Active Parenting model of parenting derived from the theories of Alfred Adler and Rudolf Dreikurs, two of the truly great psychological thinkers of the twentieth century. Their principles and methods have proven effective with millions of parents and educators, and the field of parent education is greatly in their debt. To complement the Adlerian base of this program we have included work derived from communication theorists such as Tom Gordon, Carl Rogers, Robert Carkuff, and Haim Ginott. The combination of such "empathy training" and Adlerian parenting methods represents a powerful parenting model. The original Active Parenting program and its companion program, *Active Parenting of Teens*, along with their revisions, have been used successfully by millions of parents all over the world since 1983.

To my parents, Harry and Naomi Popkin, my wife, Melody, and children, Megan and Benjamin. Thank you once again for your support and involvement in this project, and most of all, for your love.

A huge acknowledgement to the staff of Active Parenting, with special thanks to Molly McBride, Product Development Manager, and her team, who kept the project moving forward in fine fashion. Gabrielle Tingley's artistic talent, Rhea Lewis-Ngcobo's impeccable attention to detail, and Virginia Murray's practical wisdom helped to make this program one of which we can be proud.

From Elizabeth Einstein: In adapting the Active Parenting program to support stepfamilies, I appreciated the research of several talented scholars: Dr. Patricia Papernow, the first to present an insightful model of stepfamily development; Dr. Kay Pasley, Dr. Mary Whiteside, Dr. James Bray and others who contributed to stepfamily literature. The stepfamily movement began in the early 1980s when Drs. Emily and John Visher wrote the first book for professionals and formed the national Stepfamily Association of America. Their dedication made a vast difference to millions of stepfamilies. I've adapted their work on stepfamily structure and boundary issues and owe them much for supporting my career. Great gratitude to my mentor, the late Virginia Satir, a communications master who guided my thinking about the need for time, process, and creativity when working with all families.

To cousin Steve Weyer, who created the stepfamily crossword. To all my children: Christopher and Jeffrey; Cynthia and Lynn; Beverly, Brenda and Kurt. Thanks for all we've learned together—that a family isn't just bound through biology but by love.

- Michael Popkin & Elizabeth Einstein, 2007

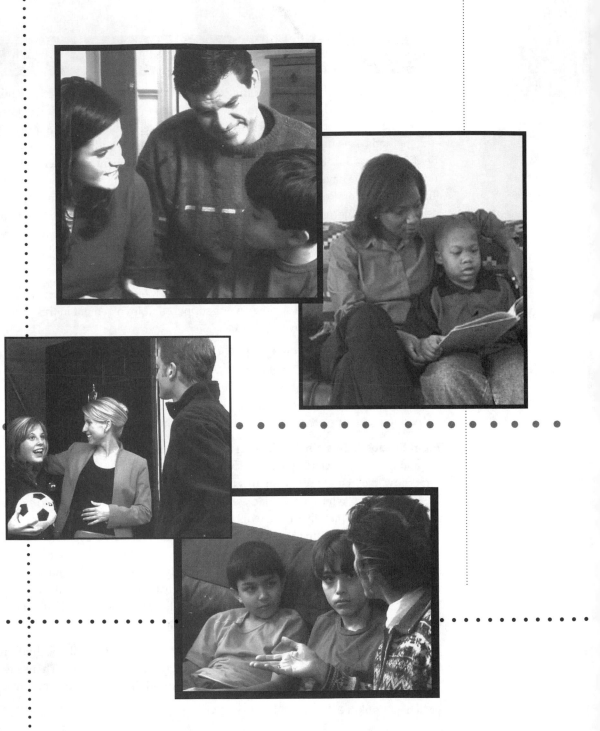

Introduction
The Active Parent in a Changing World

Parenting, though still one of the most underrated jobs in our society, is beginning to attract some of the attention and consideration it deserves. After all, if the future of our society is our children, then the key to that future rests primarily with parents and teachers. Many schools, religious institutions, mental health centers, and other community organizations are responding to this reality by offering classes and programs to parents.

Parenting in a stepfamily introduces a host of new challenges. Many parenting skills can be used successfully by parents in all types of families: intact families, foster families, adoptive families, and stepfamilies. Even so, it's not true that "one size fits all" with parenting programs. If you're a parent in a stepfamily, you may have had some frustrating experiences trying to apply traditional parenting skills (or simply what you already know about parenting) to the complexities of stepfamily living. In truth, parenting in a stepfamily requires a combination of traditional parenting skills and specialized knowledge that takes into account how stepfamilies are different.

This guide is for both biological parents and stepparents either already in a stepfamily or thinking about starting one. Whether the stepparent is or is not also a biological parent, this guide will help. It's for the "other" biological parent, as well: for example, the single divorced mother who is concerned about how her former husband's stepfamily will affect their shared children. This guide is for grandparents, aunts and uncles, and anyone who feels responsible for the well being of children in a stepfamily. It's also for foster and adoptive parents, who share many of the challenges that parents in stepfamilies face.

The Purpose of Parenting

While most everyone can agree that stepfamily parenting comes with its own unique set of challenges, few really know what to expect when starting a stepfamily, especially with regard to parenting.

Success at any job requires a sound understanding of its purpose. The basic purpose of parenting has not changed throughout history, and it's as true in stepfamilies as it is in traditional families:

>*The purpose of parenting is to protect and prepare our children to survive and thrive in the kind of society in which they live.*

Although the purpose of parenting has not changed over the years, our society has changed in the following ways:

It's more dangerous. The illegal drugs available to today's children and teens are easier to find and more harmful than ever. Crimes against children—and by children—are more numerous than when you were growing up. Although schools are generally safe places for kids, the reality of school violence has shaken our sense of security. And the risk of terrorism is something we're all concerned about. Even sexual activity can now be life threatening.

This poses a difficult problem for parents. Part of your purpose is to protect your children so they'll survive. Yet if you overprotect them, you're not preparing them to thrive on their own. Keep in mind that the job of parenting is to work yourself out of a job! That means preparing your children for independence. Three things will help you do this:

1. **Talk with other adults to get an idea of what risks are reasonable for your children to take in your community.** For example, how old should they be before you leave them home alone? Where is it safe for them to play?

2. **Join with associations, parent or stepfamily support groups, or other organizations.** Work within your community to make it a better place for children.

3. **Allow your children to develop independence gradually.** *Active Parenting for Stepfamilies* will help you learn the skills that will encourage the children in your stepfamily to become successfully independent. Because children develop through various stages, appropriate behavior at one age may not be appropriate at another. Many good books are available to help you know what to expect at these ages and stages of development. Talking with your child's teachers and other parents will help you, too. Understanding age-appropriate behavior and stepkids' special needs is essential for stepfamily adults who have no prior parenting experience. It will help them hold more realistic expectations about their new stepchildren.

Society is more diverse and more just. If the bad news about modern society is that it has become more dangerous, the good news is that it has also become more just. We can be proud that our country was founded on the principle that all people are created equal.[1] In fact, this concept of equality is a hallmark of democratic societies throughout the world. Unfortunately, the word "all" in the United States of America in 1776 really meant all white males who owned land. The rest were not even allowed to vote. But the ball of social progress was rolling, and during the next 150 years, such milestones as the end of slavery, the beginning of the labor movement, and the right of women to vote showed that we intended to fulfill the promise of democracy. With the advent of television in the 1950s, the movement for social equality took a giant leap forward. When Martin Luther King, Jr. spoke of his dream of equality for all humankind, the ever-present eye of the camera carried his message throughout the world. One group after another—African-Americans, Native Americans, Hispanics, Asians, women, students—began to demand that they, too, be treated as equals. Today, no group wants to be treated as inferior, to unquestioningly do what they are told, to speak only when spoken to, or to otherwise allow disrespectful treatment.

The atmosphere of equality in which our children live has created a new challenge for today's active parents. Many young people are no longer

---

1   Because *Active Parenting For Stepfamilies* was first published in the United States, historical references refer to this democratic society. Because each democratic society has its own story to tell, parents in countries other than the U.S. may wish to share ways in which their own struggle for equality was achieved.

comfortable with their traditional role of social inferiority. Today's children don't want to be "seen and not heard". They want to be respected as equals.

The parenting skills taught in this book reflect the need for new approaches to leadership in a society of equals. However, the concept that "all (people) are created equal" does not mean that all people are created the same. Differences between people range from the obvious, such as how we look, to the subtle, such as our dreams and values. People also have different roles in society and different responsibilities depending on those roles.

In spite of these differences, we're all considered of equal value and worth under our American Constitution. This means we're entitled to equal protection under the law, equal opportunity for employment, a right to make our opinions known, and many others.

Parents and children are equal in some ways and different in others. One big way that they're different is in their family roles. The parent's role is that of a teacher or leader, while the child is often in the role of student or learner. As the leaders in the family, parents have different rights and responsibilities than their children. For example, parents have the responsibility of providing food, clothing, shelter, and protection for their children. They also have the legal rights to drive, vote, use alcohol, and exercise other privileges that children don't have.

In addition, parents have the authority to decide many matters that affect the lives of their children, including issues of health, safety, spirituality, and family values. In this guide, we'll take a close look at the issues surrounding parental authority in stepfamilies.

Society changes at an increasing rate. Today's high-tech society changes faster than any in history. Jobs, even industries, that thrive in one decade may be gone the next, replaced by new technologies that were undiscovered when you were in school. Success in such a high-change society requires children to adapt to change and keep learning. Neither blind obedience nor an attitude of complacency is likely to provide them with the skills and character necessary to adapt successfully to inevitable social and environmental changes.

This guide will help you learn how to empower your children to be effective decision makers, problem solvers, team players, lifelong learners, and eventually mates and parents—all within the context of stepfamily life in our fast-changing society.

Family composition has changed. As is evident by the existence of this program, change in society has also affected the structure of families. The traditional nuclear family of two biological parents and their biological children is no longer the norm; alternate family structures are now more common than traditional types. More than half of all children will find themselves living in divorced or widowed families or stepfamilies. Many other children will live with

grandparents, same-gender parents, or caregivers with whom they share no previous ties at all, such as adoptive and foster parents. No matter what your family type, but especially if your family has undergone changes in its structure, the skills in this book will help you develop the kind of relationship you and your children need to thrive now and later.

The Risks: Drugs, Sexuality, and Violence

Kids in all modern families face risks that are usually alien to the adults in their family. Effective co-parents will learn what these risks are and how to guard kids, marriages, and family integrity against them.

The risks associated with drugs, sexuality, and violence are greatest during the teen years. However, what you do now as parents and stepparents will make a huge difference in what your children will do later when you're not around. We'll focus on four ways to help protect your kids against these risks:

1. Build character and develop skills in your children.

Using the active parenting skills in this guide will help build five important personal traits in your kids: courage, self-esteem, responsibility, cooperation, and respect. This guide will also help you develop in your children the personal skills that they will need to succeed—including problem solving, communication, anger management, healthy grieving, and the means for achieving academic success. By developing these traits and skills, you can help your children build a strong foundation from which they can resist easy answers to life's problems. These easy answers might include smoking, drinking alcohol, using drugs, or engaging in irresponsible sexuality and violent behavior.

2. Build strong relationships with your kids.

Your ability to influence the values that the kids in your life will form and the decisions they'll make is, to a large extent, dependent on the quality of your relationship with them. Child-adult relationships in typical stepfamilies are often stressful, especially soon after new mates start living together. If the relationship is mostly negative, kids often reject even your good ideas. They're quick to rebel and to prove that you can't push them around.

Sometimes this rebellion takes the form of drug use, irresponsible sexuality, and violence as they intentionally reject your values in these matters. The active model of parenting that you'll be learning in this program minimizes these risks while still empowering you and your partner to be the leaders in the family and to build strong parent-child relationships.

3. Become aware of your own psychological wounds.

Often, kids who make self-destructive choices come from families where conflict prevents nurturing from being a priority. Their parents have often inherited psychological wounds from their own childhoods. These parents may unknowingly continue the negative cycle by choosing a partner who is also psychologically wounded.

Once partners are aware of this harmful cycle, they can take specific steps to spot and reduce any wounds they bear. Once they convert unawareness into knowledge, they can begin to convert knowledge into action, working together to stop the negative cycle.

4. Talk persuasively about the risks.

Once you've laid the groundwork for a positive relationship with each of the children in your stepfamily, it's important to talk to them about the specific risks involved with drugs, irresponsible sexuality, and violence. You'll want to be as persuasive as possible in making your case and winning over their attitudes, because attitude is what will ultimately determine what they do. Discipline can be helpful, but discipline alone is not enough to win the battle for their minds. We'll discuss effective communication skills in

Chapter 2 and encourage you to use these skills when you talk with your children about risks and important issues in their lives. The more you can enrich your relationships with your children and stepchildren, the more they'll allow you to be an influence in their lives.

It's All About Character

Because you won't always be there to ensure that your children and stepchildren make good decisions, it's essential that they develop an underlying framework of beliefs, attitudes, and values that will help them steer a successful course on their own. We commonly refer to this underlying framework as "character," and it's one of the most important concepts in parenting. Even if you're a new stepparent who wasn't involved in your stepchildren's character development up to now, it's now your responsibility to start doing this important work. Your success depends on the strength of your relationships with the children. This is true of all types of parents, step and biological included.

Although there are many traits that you'll want to instill in your children and stepchildren, we think there are five that are especially critical for success in today's high-tech, diverse, and democratic society:

Courage is the first. The psychologist Alfred Adler once said that if he could give one gift to a child, it would be courage. If a child is courageous, he reasoned, that child can learn everything else she needs to learn. Coupled with parental guidance, a child's courage enables her to try, fail, and try again, until she masters the challenges life presents. Courage can also give a child the ability to admit when she has made a mistake so that she can then move on to learn from it. With too little courage, the child gives up easily or doesn't try at all. Fear leads to failure, and failure reinforces fear. Such a cycle of discouragement supports a lifelong attitude of regret and resentment. Courage is a foundation upon which the child constructs her personality. It's at the heart of human potential. Because we consider courage to be so essential to a child's development, we devote much of Chapter 5 to methods of encouraging children, and we'll be referring to courage again and again.

Self-esteem is the second quality necessary for thriving in our changing society and the dynamic stepfamily environment. Simply stated, self-esteem is the opinion we have of ourselves. When a child's self-esteem is high, he sees himself as a capable human being who has a good opportunity to succeed at challenges. He also knows that even "failure" is always a chance to *learn*, so when he doesn't succeed at first, he doesn't give up. The perception of himself as a winner gives the child the courage to tackle life's problems through positive behavior and to take advantage of the wonderful opportunities available in a democratic society. We'll explore the critical connection between self-esteem, courage, and behavior in Chapter 5.

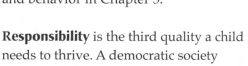

Responsibility is the third quality a child needs to thrive. A democratic society demands that its members make decisions and accept responsibility for the consequences of those decisions. Without individual responsibility, our cherished freedoms will give way to governmental responsibility, where the state will make decisions for us.

With freedom and choice comes the responsibility for the consequences of those choices. The reality of our society is that its children will be called upon to make thousands of choices, and they will be held responsible for their choices by experiencing the consequences that follow. Some of these choices will be life and death matters. They'll be offered drugs; will they choose to accept? They'll face choices about drinking, sex, crime, dropping out of school, and even suicide. And their parents won't always be there to tell them what to do. But if they have been taught to make responsible decisions and have developed the courage to stand behind these decisions, they'll be prepared to meet these challenges. We'll explore ways to teach responsibility throughout the program and especially in Chapter 3.

Cooperation is the fourth essential quality that children should develop. Some people advocate competition as the road to success. In reality, teamwork is what moves society forward. Helping a child learn that they should strive not to be dependent nor independent, but to be interdependent, is a cornerstone of *Active Parenting for Stepfamilies*. In a society of equals, cooperation skills have high value, and the child who *wants* to cooperate is far more likely to thrive than one who has never learned how. Ideally, parent-child relationships are basically cooperative rather than competitive. But parents and stepparents cannot demand cooperation from a child, especially when new stepfamily ties have resulted in strained relationships. Like respect and trust, cooperation must be earned. In each session of this program, we'll offer ways of achieving cooperative relationships between parent and child through Stepfamily Enrichment Activities. In addition, much of Chapter 2 is devoted to teaching ways of winning cooperation through effective communication skills.

Respect is the fifth quality that we'll address, and we'll be starting in the first chapter because respect is the cornerstone of life in a democratic society. Teaching children to respect themselves and others begins at home, but it pays dividends in every aspect of their lives. Respect is about appreciating the worthwhile qualities in ourselves and others and demonstrating this through actions as well as attitude.

· · · · · · · · ·

These five character traits are essential for adults, as well. In fact, as parents and stepparents in the challenging environment of a stepfamily, you'll often draw from the strength of your character to deal with conflict, solve problems, and work on relationships with your children and stepchildren. The active parenting skills taught throughout this program are powered by your own courage, self-esteem, responsibility, cooperation, and respect. These traits can also lend strength to your couple relationship. In each chapter, a Marriage Enrichment Activity will offer a new way to strengthen that bond.

Stepfamily Living:
A Different Parenting Challenge

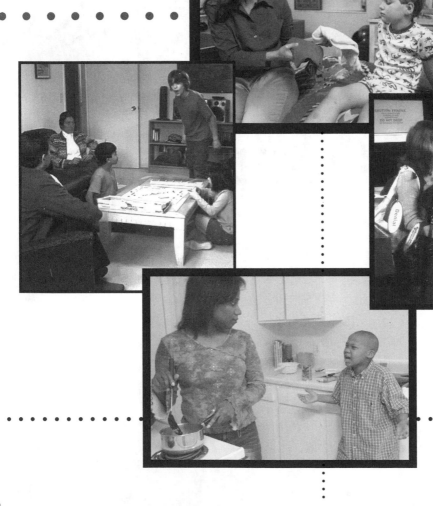

If you're already in a stepfamily, you've known from the start that your family is different. Maybe you couldn't put your finger on exactly how, but you knew that things you did in your first family didn't always work in your new one—especially when it came to parenting.

Parenting is a tremendously "active" undertaking, requiring a 24/7 commitment and a myriad of skills ranging from discipline to communication and support. Parenting requires a lot of energy! It becomes even more challenging in a stepfamily, with more people and more complex issues. Since children respond better to actions than to words, an effective parent is an active parent. This is one of the reasons we have chosen the name *Active Parenting for Stepfamilies* for this guide.

Since children respond better to actions than to words, an effective parent is an active parent.

We also think of the word *active* as a contrast to the *reactive* approach used by many parents. Reactive parents wait until their children push them to their limits, and then they react, often with frustration, anger, and random discipline… or as one mother put it, "the screech and hit" school of parenting. When parents react rather than act, they are allowing the child to control both the situation and the parent's own emotions. Problems tend to continue or even worsen as parent and child reenact the same frustrating scenes over and over.

Part of the problem is that most parents do not have a consistent approach to parenting. They use a little of what their parents did, a little of the exact opposite of what their parents did, and a little of what they picked up from friends, books, and magazine articles. This guide will help you clarify goals for your children and will teach you effective methods for leading them toward those goals. It will also teach you a consistent model of parenting that enables you to act with confidence and clarity as you encounter the many challenges of parenting in a stepfamily. Because the typical stepfamily differs greatly from the intact ("traditional") family, effective parenting often requires an approach that's different from what you may be used to. This guide will help you master these situations. Throughout the book, we'll use the term *parent* to refer to both biological parents and stepparents, unless a situation is specific to a stepparent's role.

There are more reasons we chose to emphasize the word "active" in this guide. This is an age in which people are engaged in a host of active pursuits: jobs and careers, community work, political causes, the arts, hobbies, sports, and—last but definitely not least—family. The fact that you are reading this book shows that you are one of these active people. You're one who is taking steps toward improving your family interactions, and you're seeking information to help you excel as a parent. So *Active Parenting for Stepfamilies* is for people like you.

A word of caution: The parenting model presented in this guide has been used effectively by millions of parents, counselors, teachers and psychologists. It works! However, it is put into use by imperfect human beings. We all make mistakes. During this workshop you'll probably become aware of two kinds of mistakes of your own:

First, you may realize or recall mistakes you or your former spouse made as parents in the past. If you do, let them go. They're in the past, and it's useless to dwell on them now. The same goes for your children and stepchildren's mistakes: put them in the past. It's much more productive to concentrate on being a more effective parent in the present and the future.

Second, you and your new partner will make further mistakes as you learn these new skills. Mistakes promote learning. They happen to everyone using new skills. So help each other accept your parenting mistakes without punishing yourselves, because criticism tends to make people defensive. Soon you won't want to admit your mistakes even to yourself, and you'll lose the valuable opportunity to correct and improve your performance. Remind each other that mistakes are for learning, so please be gentle with yourselves when you make them!

What Makes Stepfamilies Different?

What are some of the early challenges that make parenting more difficult in stepfamilies? Many of these challenges are similar to those in foster and adoptive families. Significant change and loss have played a large role in these families. It's critical that parents in stepfamilies understand how change and grief have shaped their children's lives—and their own lives—up to now.

Many newly remarried couples have a trio of troublesome issues they haven't cleared up: unresolved loss, unrealistic expectations, and lack of preparation for the coming changes. Too soon, the excitement and joy from the wedding wear off, and these unresolved issues begin to play themselves out, creating challenges that make it harder for you to get your new family on a successful path. Let's see how these challenges could compromise your ability to parent effectively and build relationships in your stepfamily.

Stepfamily Challenge #1: Healing from Loss

Stepfamilies are created out of loss, either through death or divorce, or even when an "unofficial" stepfamily forms after a separation. The experience of such loss often leaves behind painful emotions that may take a long time to resolve. Adults' feelings of guilt, anger, and sadness may point to unresolved grief. They might not know how to grieve because they never learned. If you haven't taken the time to grieve, chances are that your children are withholding painful feelings, as well. In fact, even if you have worked through your grief, your children may still be grieving. Each stepfamily child and adult has a different mix of losses to mourn and a unique way and pace of grieving. A death of a parent or a divorce is a loss that, in some ways, can affect children's lives forever. The many changes they've experienced as their family reorganized may have left them confused. The most major change for children is that they no longer see both parents daily. Maybe they moved and left familiar surroundings—their own room, neighborhood friends, school. Perhaps they lived in a single parent family for a while and got used to their role and the expectations in that family.

Now, with remarriage, their family has changed once again. Children may wonder where they fit in, how to relate to this new adult in their lives, and what will happen to them. This mixture of past and present loss and change may confuse your children and stepchildren—and even contribute to their misbehavior.

Stages of Grief

While recovering from an important loss, sometimes called "grief work," a person moves through at least three separate stages: shock, pain (plus denial), and acceptance.

The first stage, **shock**, is characterized by a sense of disbelief that this is really happening. "I can't believe they are really getting a divorce. How can this be happening to <u>us</u>?" There may be an accompanying sense of panic about what the future will bring and how one will cope.

As reality sinks in and the person begins to experience the **pain** of stage two (sadness, anger, guilt, fear, and other hurtful emotions), a **denial** mechanism is often triggered. The child or adult may tell himself and others that he is okay and has accepted the divorce (or death) and moved on.

Denial can appear in several forms:

Denying the importance of grieving loss and change. Some people deny to themselves the importance of grieving and accepting the losses experienced with their former families. They may find it appealing to remarry without completing the grieving process. Beware of this temptation. When you suppress the great sadness of saying goodbye to your family as it once was, unresolved grief may rear its head in your new family as anger, depression, or guilt. If you unconsciously direct these feelings at your partner or stepchildren, it makes forming new relationships very difficult. And if you don't help children deal with the immense loss that preceded the formation of your stepfamily, they may not bond well with new stepparents.

When you suppress the great sadness of saying goodbye to your family as it once was, unresolved grief may rear its head in your new family as anger, depression, or guilt.

Denying the importance of your former partner. Some adults deny the importance of a former spouse to their children's lives, or they deny stepchildren's need to maintain positive relationships with their other biological parent. When children of divorce have poor or no relationships with their biological parents, they have far greater problems adjusting to their remarriage and their new stepparent.

Denying the feelings of family members. Anger, fear, jealousy, guilt, shame, confusion, and resentment are all normal in new stepfamilies. So is denying or minimizing these painful feelings. But when family members don't talk openly about these feelings and allow them to be expressed, the result is often even greater conflict and stress. Make it okay in your family to feel whatever it is that you or your children are feeling, and model to your children how to express these painful feelings in words, rather than through misbehavior. The skills presented in this guide will help.

If your remarriage is to succeed, you must move beyond denial. It merely dulls the pain and hinders your progression through the healing process. Denial cannot erase your feelings, and continued denial dents your chances for a successful stepfamily. To move out of denial, try these specific steps:

1. **Create awareness.** Recognize that some stressful issues and strong feelings exist among the members of your stepfamily—as in all families. Admit your own part in upholding the denial and your motive in doing so. Imagine your own worst fear of exposure, and begin to face that fear.

2. **Make new decisions.** Awareness alone isn't enough. Family members must risk sharing their fears and feelings to air long-denied issues. Family meetings, as recommended throughout this guide, offer a

positive and safe environment for this. Another way to vent feelings is in a stepfamily support group where you will learn that you aren't alone in your struggles, and that there's nothing wrong with *you*. If your family problems are severe, find a professional who has been trained to understand the special dynamics of stepfamilies.

3. **Practice communicating honestly.** To reduce denial in your stepfamily, adults must actively promote continual sharing of thoughts, feelings, and needs among family members. For many, this is threatening and risky, but encouraging them to practice sharing in a safe and accepting environment will eventually help them replace the negative associations with positive ones.

Cutting through denial means feeling some pain, but it opens the door to stage three of the grieving process: **acceptance**. As children and parents are able to release their painful emotions, a sense of hope emerges, and they begin to believe that life can still be good. They may still feel a little sad about their loss, but a new attitude of acceptance replaces the deep pain associated with stage two. A person who has reached this stage often grows even stronger through the experience and is able to use the lessons learned from it to live a fuller life.

Emotional Baggage

Adults bring to new relationships many unresolved issues having to do with their upbringing, their self-esteem, their regrets and hopes, their previous relationships, and many other factors. We all have such issues, but when they remain unknown to us, they can create significant family role and relationship problems. We call this batch of unresolved issues *emotional baggage* because we tend to carry it with us wherever we go. This unwieldy load can weigh down your stepfamily. Ask yourself a few of the following questions to find out more about the "baggage" that you carried to your remarriage:

What is the quality of your relationship with your parents—your first models for marriage?

Is communication between you and other family members clear and comfortable, or is it confusing and tense?

Are you aware of any active addictions, like alcoholism, smoking, eating disorders, overworking?

Do you have cut-off relationships— people with whom you don't communicate at all—in your family of origin?

What is the ongoing quality of relationship that you have with your former partner?

That last question is vital. [2] Explore it further by asking yourself:

Do you and your former partner still argue rather than work cooperatively to solve problems?

Do you have ongoing legal disputes?

Have you forgiven yourselves and each other?

Do you act and speak respectfully about each other to your children, stepchildren, new partner, relatives, and friends?

The relationship you have with your former partner is critical to your stepfamily. Kids must be able to move between these two homes comfortably, and the adults must be able to negotiate parenting issues clearly. If you and your children's other biological parent remain in conflict, your children will feel torn between loyalties to each of you, making parenting more difficult and straining your relationship with your new partner. Loyalty conflicts undermine your children's self-esteem and cause confusion, jealousy, guilt, and resentment—feelings that can easily translate

2   If you find yourself in moderate to severe conflict with your former partner, we recommend that you use a program called *Cooperative Parenting and Divorce*, available from Active Parenting Publishers. This program will help you learn how to put your children's needs first as you make the transition from an unsuccessful marital relationship to a successful co-parenting relationship.

into troublesome behavior. For example, kids might not be able to relate appropriately to new stepparents because they are consumed by worries such as… *If I learn to like my new stepmother, will my own mother be sad? Hurt? Jealous? Angry with me?*

Stepfamily Challenge #2: Exploring Expectations

All of us hold expectations about how things should be in our families as well as in our relationships, our careers, and elsewhere. Expectations are especially important in stepfamilies, because there are so many new roles— stepsister, half brother, step-grandmother, non-custodial father—with which family members have little experience. But unless family members talk with each other about what they expect regarding responsibility, behaviors, choices, communication, or how to fulfill individual and family needs, expectations may remain unmet, leading to frustration, anger, and conflict between family members.

Expectations can cause serious trouble in new stepfamilies because everyone and everything is new to one another.

Expectations can cause serious trouble in new stepfamilies because everyone and everything is new to one another. Just putting two families in the same household doesn't mean everyone's going to think or behave the way you've come to expect in a former family. New mates need to clarify and agree on their long-range personal, marital, and family priorities. This is the basis for starting out strongly as a stepfamily, and it's best done during courtship, but if you did not make time for it before the wedding, "as soon as possible" is better than "not at all."

Here are some questions to get a conversation about expectations started with your partner (best done before remarriage):

How are you accustomed to disciplining your children?

What are your goals for your children?

Do you make it a priority with your kids to keep the house tidy?

How do you handle giving your children spending money?

Once both of you have discussed your individual expectations, it's time to devise a new set. This means adjusting "my" expectations to "our" expectations. Begin this process by taking inventory of the major differences between your expectations and your spouse's. Then, work together to answer this question:

How can we cooperate to create the "united front" that is necessary to parent our children effectively and prepare them for the future?

Even more troublesome are *unrealistic expectations*. You may have unspoken hopes about how you want your stepchildren to relate to you and how you should parent them. It's tempting to tell yourself that these expectations are both realistic and in line with your partner's, but if you don't talk about it with each other, you risk igniting a major conflict. When the children behave differently than you'd hoped or expected, you may feel angry or hurt—even rejected. You and your partner might argue about whose expectations are realistic, a debate that becomes more bitter when it occurs after damage has already been done. So give yourself a "reality check" by discussing your expectations with your partner. Cooperation and good communication can help you see which ones are more realistic and which need some adjustment. Although it might hurt to discover that your partner thinks your expectations are unrealistic, by listening with an open mind you'll, avoid more serious problems in the future.

Although it might hurt to discover that your partner thinks your expectations are unrealistic, by listening with an open mind, you'll avoid more serious problems in the future.

A *hidden agenda* is another kind of unrealistic expectation. Do you have a plan for your stepfamily that you haven't discussed openly with your partner? For example, maybe parenting as a single parent was especially hard for you as you tried to juggle work, kids, family, and a personal life. You're relieved that someone new is on board to help you with the parenting task or even take over for you. If you haven't discussed this with your partner, it's a hidden agenda. Your partner may have a parenting style that's incompatible with your unspoken plan—an incompatibility that could potentially upset the entire family.

Often we develop expectations of other people because we have a goal in mind, based on our own needs. Even an unrealistic parenting expectation may be rooted in a seemingly reasonable goal that you and your spouse agree on. For example, you two may share the goal of building trusting relationships among all stepfamily members, but you might have different ideas about how to achieve this goal. You might expect your spouse to take charge of the relationship-building effort; your spouse, on the other hand, might expect you to smooth the way. In other words, it's the lack of clarity about expectations that causes the conflict. In the chart on the next page, you can see how an unrealistic expectation can sabotage a stepfamily's progress toward achieving a parenting goal. But you'll also see that by adopting a more realistic expectation, the outcome becomes positive.

The closeness that you and your partner can gain from working out expectations together will help strengthen the very foundation of your stepfamily: your marriage.

Many adults postpone or neglect to discuss their expectations about parenting and discipline openly with their spouse because they fear that doing so might uncover differences that could end the relationship. Such conversations don't feel very romantic, but they are essential—especially discussions that involve parenting issues, because parenting will become your number one challenge in the stepfamily. The closeness that you and your partner can gain from working out expectations together will help strengthen the very foundation of your stepfamily: your marriage.

Unrealistic vs. Realistic Expectations

Unrealistic Expectation	Parenting Goal	Negative Outcome	Realistic Expectation	Positive Outcome
Biological mom wants new stepfather to take over discipline ASAP.	Regain control over the kids after they've gotten used to living with few rules in a single-parent home.	Kids rebel, saying, "You're not my father. I don't have to do what you say."	New stepfather takes on nurturing role early and waits to earn trust and authority with stepchildren before trying to discipline.	Stepfather will gradually get to know his new stepchildren as he builds bonds and earns their trust.
Stepmother defends stepson's misbehavior (in front of the child) after child's bio-father makes a rule to prohibit that misbehavior.	Make my stepson like/love me.	Sabotages bio-father's authority, confuses the child, triggers a loyalty conflict, creates tension in the couple relationship.	Establish a clear, effective parenting plan before conflict arises. In this case, Stepmom could speak privately with her husband rather than disagreeing with him in stepson's presence.	Effective co-parenting is modeled. Stepchild is more responsive.
Parenting problems won't take long to resolve.	Become a stable stepfamily as soon as possible.	Children are angry and resentful about differences and changes. They blame stepparent for problems.	Commit to creating a joint, effective parenting plan to be carried out over time.	Children feel secure and can bond with their stepparent at their own pace. Adults feel confident about parenting.
Stepchildren should learn to do things your way.	Get a task done.	Stepchildren resent their way being judged as wrong. They become angry and resentful, and they may rebel.	Accept that the stepchildren want to continue with their way of doing things. Suggest a compromise to create a new way.	Stepchildren feel accepted by new stepparent, the first step toward building bonds.
Parents disagree about how to discipline the children.	Get the kids shaped up.	Confusion and lack of clarity for the children lead to misbehavior.	Parents need to present a "united front" about discipline to be effective.	Children feel safe and secure within a strong remarriage.

Chart adapted with permission from *Strengthening Your Stepfamily* (by Einstein and Albert, *Impact Publishers*, 2006).

Stepfamily Challenge #3: Adapting to Change

As you've learned, unresolved grief and unrealistic expectations can get your stepfamily off to a rough start. So can a third issue: the experience of rapid change that your family has undergone. Adults and children often lack information about how stepfamilies differ, so they jump into the challenge of stepfamily living unprepared, and they encounter problems that could have been avoided. It's never too late to learn. Above all, you need to understand and adapt to the fact that your new stepfamily is different in two major ways: in its development and in its structure.

1. **Development** The process of developing a cohesive, well-functioning stepfamily takes *years*. While your wedding ceremony created an "instant family," there's nothing "instant" about building good relationships and a sense of unity within that family. It's important that you accept this reality so that you don't give up too soon.

2. **Structure** This refers to your family's make-up—its shape—and how it works within that context. The shape of the once-familiar traditional family included one mother, one father, and their children all living in the same household, maybe with a pet or two. There were two sets of grandparents. Everyone understood the roles and rules. But your new stepfamily shape looks very different. There may be two sets of parents with new partners who become stepparents, at least four sets of grandparents, and all of the children living in multiple households.

Other structural differences make a stepfamily unlike traditional families, as well: no legal relationships exist between stepparents and stepchildren; children often move between their biological parents' houses; the new family has to face many loss issues early on; and finally, the strength of your new couple bond isn't nearly as powerful as the bond between biological parents and their children. This last difference alone can cause many loyalty conflicts.

Responding to these three challenges—healing from loss, exploring expectations, and adapting to change—requires clear priorities, flexibility, and effective communication. You can't change the past, and you can't control the future. What you *can* do is to learn ways to make the present better and better. Sometimes this means having the courage to stand firm, and other times to willingly compromise. The skills you will be learning in this program will help. Your positive attitude will help, too.

Styles of Parenting

Your goal as a parent is to instill in your children the skills and character that enable them to survive and thrive in our fast-changing, diverse, democratic society. You and your partner share the responsibility—and the authority—to get the job done. However, there's not much use being a leader if no one is willing to follow you. Here, then, is an important principle of leadership:

> *Leaders get their ultimate authority*
> *from those they lead.*

There's not much use being a leader if no one is willing to follow you.

The same is true for parents in stepfamilies. You may be the authorities in your families, but to be effective, you must have the cooperation of your children and stepchildren. As a stepparent, your parenting authority is somewhat different from that of a biological parent, because it can take a long time to develop genuine acceptance and cooperation from typical stepchildren—especially if they have unresolved grief from their prior losses. Not only is the trust-earning part of the equation more complex for stepparents, but you might also find that your stepchildren's biological parents want you to play a small part while they take the leading role as family authoritarian. Leadership is a complicated issue in stepfamilies. The adults in the family need to come to an agreement about how the family leadership should be distributed. It ultimately involves transferring some authority to the stepparent. We'll discuss this in depth in Chapter 4.

Let's look at three types of leadership and compare their effectiveness in our society and in a stepfamily.

1. Autocratic Style: The Dictator

A **dictator** is one who has absolute control, and the autocratic parent is all-powerful in dictating the lives of his or her children. This parent is a dominating figure who rewards and punishes to enforce his orders. Children are told what to do, how to do it, and when to do it. There is little or no room for them to question, challenge, or disagree. The dictator method of parenting worked reasonably well in times when inequality was normal between people, but it works poorly in today's time of equality.

Children who grow up in autocratic families seldom thrive. Either they have their spirits broken and give up or, more often, they rebel. This rebellion usually happens during the teen years because the child has developed enough power to fight back. The dictator has been the typical parenting style for so many generations that teenage rebellion has come to be accepted by many experts as "normal." This is a mistake. Teenagers do not have to rebel to become independent.

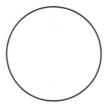

The **dictator** or **authoritarian** style can be described as **"limits without freedom."** This style can be depicted as a closed circle.

To his credit, the dictator does understand the need children have for limits. He has the emotional strength and willingness to get involved and to stand firm. But he often goes too far.

You are tending toward the autocratic style of parenting when you say things like:

"Because I said so!"

"I'm your stepfather now, and as long as you live under my roof, you'll obey my rules."

"When you are the parent, you can decide what to do."

…and when you do things like:

- *Tell your stepchild what to wear.*

- *Find yourself angry and yelling often.*

- *Often ground or punish your child in other ways.*

2. Permissive Style: The Doormat

Permissive parents often react strongly against the harsh and uncompromising autocratic method. Permissive parents allow their children to "do their own thing" too much of the time. In such households, there is little respect for order and routine, and few limits are placed on anyone's freedom. Many such parents behave like doormats, allowing their children to walk all over them. Some of these parents want to be firmer but do not know how to assert their needs and set and enforce limits effectively. Divorced parents may feel unresolved guilt about having put their kids through so much loss and change, so they try to compensate by being overly permissive. Whatever justification they give, permissive parents aren't doing their children a favor. A major drawback of this style is the feeling of insecurity that plagues children reared this way. Another is disrespect for their parents. Such children have little sense of belonging and are often hard to live with because they haven't learned to cooperate.

Children with permissive parents are often pampered and accustomed to getting their own way. When someone outside the family finally tells them that rules apply to them also, these children or teens frequently rebel. It's difficult to get a child who's used to a lifestyle with no limits to voluntarily begin obeying rules. Although the permissive parent's desire to share power with their children and allow them freedom of choice is well meant, often they go too far.

The **permissive** or **doormat** approach can be described as **"freedom without limits"** and can be shown as a squiggly line representing freedom run rampant.

You are tending towards the permissive style of parenting when you say things like:

"I don't think that's a good idea…but, well…okay, if you really want to."

"So your dad wouldn't give you the money when you were at his house? Oh, all right. I will."

"I sure wish you'd help out around here."

…and when you do things like:

- *Allow your stepdaughter to go to bed whenever she feels like it.*

- *Routinely do her homework with her or go to school to intervene for her often.*

- *Give in to her unreasonable demands because you're afraid she'll become sad or angry and think you're a mean stepparent.*

Stepfamily parents risk being overly permissive from fear of losing a child's love or failure to win over a stepchild. Then, when they begin feeling taken advantage of, they may become angry and flip into an autocratic style. We'll suggest other, better ways to develop a strong bond with your children and stepchildren later in this chapter.

3. Authoritative Style: The Active Parent

The **authoritative** style is, in some respects, the middle ground between the autocratic and permissive styles, but it is also much more. In an active household, freedom is an ideal, but so are the rights of others and the responsibilities of all. Parents are leaders who encourage mutual respect and cooperation and stimulate learning. There is order and routine in the home, and every person is an important member of the family.

The active parent acknowledges our democratic heritage and the role of social equality among all human beings in two important ways:

1. **Children should be treated with dignity and respect, even when their parents discipline them.**

2. **Children are entitled to respectfully express their thoughts and feelings to their parents.** In this way they are given the right to influence the decisions that affect their lives. This is consistent with life in a democratic society:

> *Democracy does not mean you'll always get your way.*
> *It means you'll always get your say.*

 The **authoritarian** or **active** style can be called **"freedom within limits"** and can be symbolized by a squiggly line within the limits of a circle.

In fact, it could be shown as "freedom within expanding limits." As the child assumes more and more responsibility, the parent gradually expands the limits, until eventually a young adult leaving home has the same amount of independence as his parents.

You are tending toward the active style of parenting when you say things like:

"I know you're disappointed, but you can't go. Here's why…"

"Sure we can talk about it. What's your idea?"

"I know you can handle it. If you need some help, just let me know."

…and when you do things like:

- *Involve your child or stepchild in deciding who will do which family chores.*

- *Give her the full responsibility for her homework, monitoring her just a little.*

- *Show an active interest in his education by discussing his subjects with him regularly and attending school functions.*

- *Involve her in the discipline process by talking with her about your expectations and the consequences for breaking agreements.*

- *Let him know what you like about him and encourage him often.*

- *Talk with her about important topics—such as drug use, sexuality, and violence—in a calm and non-judgmental manner that helps her understand the dangers.*

Two Keys to Active Parenting: Mutual Respect and Participation

Parenting a successful stepfamily in a democratic society is like any other type of effective leadership in a democratic society. It requires *respect* for both the leader and those who are being led, and it requires their *participation* in the decision-making process. Without respect and participation, a leader will eventually find herself with a rebellion on her hands. Let's see how these two key concepts can make you a more effective parent and leader in your stepfamily (or for that matter, a more effective manager at work!)

Mutual Respect

Starting with yourself, can you think of a person of any age who does not need to feel that others genuinely value their human dignity and worth? The need to feel respected is a requirement for healthy relationships, families, and societies.

Likewise, learning to respect oneself regardless of strengths, weaknesses, family, culture, or heritage is a building block for self-esteem and success. When you show your children respect, even when you're angry or providing

When you show your children respect, even when you're angry or providing discipline, you teach them to respect themselves while demonstrating how to treat others respectfully.

discipline, you teach them to respect themselves while demonstrating how to treat others respectfully.

Respect is particularly important in stepfamilies. While developing the strong emotional ties called "love" can take a long time (and may or may not happen at all), learning to respect each other is a far more realistic goal. Treating your children and stepchildren respectfully is the best way to teach them how to treat you respectfully. As the author Bernard Malamud once wrote, "respect is what you have to have in order to get." In other words, if you want someone to treat you respectfully, you have to be willing to treat them respectfully, too.

This concept of "mutual respect," as psychologist Rudolf Dreikurs called it, is often easier said than done. Showing children respect means not yelling, cursing, name-calling, interrupting, scorning, being sarcastic, or otherwise speaking to them in ways you would not want them speaking to you. There are also countless more subtle forms of disrespect to guard against. For example, an overprotective parent who is quick to jump in to solve a child's problem—without giving her a chance to struggle to find her own solution—is sending the disrespectful message of "I don't trust you." A parent who always insists on doing what he wants and never compromises to do what the child wants is also showing disrespect.

When you catch yourself treating your children or stepchildren disrespectfully, it's wise to smile, apologize, and if appropriate, make amends.

Examples:

"I'm sorry I yelled at you. That wasn't very respectful. Let me try again more calmly to tell you why I was angry."

"I apologize for not calling to tell you I would be late. That wasn't respectful. How can I make it up to you?"

"I'm sorry I interrupted you. That was rude of me. Please tell me again."

Teaching children to respect others– despite differences and conflicts—requires that parents work to earn their kids' respect, by showing respect for them. An effective way to do this is by practicing the discipline skills we'll cover in Chapter 4. Examples:

> *"I don't talk to you that way. Please do not talk to me that way."*

> *"When you talk disrespectfully to your stepmother, I feel angry and frustrated. I need you kids to find a better way of communicating together."*

> *"I want you kids to stop right now. We don't talk to each other that way in our family."*

As we'll see in Chapter 4, when your words alone aren't enough to correct misbehavior, you'll want to use a logically connected consequence to help get your message understood.

Examples:

> *"Either talk to me without yelling or go to your room."*

> *"Either share the remote control without fighting or there will be no TV at all."*

> *"Either talk to me respectfully about not letting you watch a PG-13 movie or there will be no movies at all this week."*

Finally, the respect with which we treat our spouses, significant others, ex-spouses, and even strangers sets an example for our children. When mutual respect is a cornerstone of your own interactions with people, as well as a strong family value, your children come to adopt it almost without trying.

Participation and the Method of Choice

The second key to active parenting is to promote children's **participation** in the decisions that affect their lives. This concept is one of the single most powerful forces in existence–so powerful that nations will go to war to preserve their right to choose how to live their lives. When we say that the hallmark of the active style of parenting is "freedom within limits," what we mean is the freedom of children to participate in decisions that affect their lives.

Just as people will rise up and overthrow a dictator, children will resist parents or stepparents who rob them of their chance to participate. An active parent will use this knowledge to handle problems and teach responsibility.

One way to invite your child's participation is by using what we call **The Method of Choice**. Choice is power. As the leader of your family, you can give your children choices that are appropriate for their age and levels of responsibility. This, again, is the idea of freedom within expanding limits. The freedom to choose is tremendously

The freedom to choose is tremendously empowering to children.

empowering to children. And because you exercise your authority to respectfully limit what choices the child is allowed to make, family rules and values aren't sacrificed.

Even young children can be given simple choices. Allowing your child or stepchild the opportunity to practice decision making can become a regular part of your daily routine. This can also be useful in helping resolve conflicts. Consider this common situation of getting your child dressed:

After unsuccessfully trying to coerce Austin into wearing his yellow shirt, Katy gives Austin a choice.

> *Katy: "Would you rather wear this yellow shirt or the red one?"*
>
> *Austin: "The red one."*

This gives Austin some power over the decisions that affect his life, so he has less need to rebel. He chooses the red one, which is acceptable to Katy.

Had he chosen a shirt that was unacceptable for the situation, Katy would have limited his choice.

> *Katy: I'm sorry, Austin, the T-shirt with spaghetti stains just isn't appropriate for going out. Let's stick with these two…this white one, or this blue one.*

As children get older, the choices they are given can become more open-ended. So instead of either the blue or white shirt, you might simply ask the child what he would like to wear. The following are some examples of choices you can use.

Younger Kids	Older Kids
Do you want to wear the yellow dress or the blue dress?	Can you choose something special to wear to your stepsister's violin concert?
Which story do you want to read together: *The Velveteen Rabbit* or *Where the Wild Things Are*?	Pick out two books from the "Young Readers" section of the library.
I'd like you to help me decide which vegetable we have with dinner tonight: broccoli or green beans?	I'd like your help planning dinner this week. What would you like to have?

A word of caution: Don't get carried away and make everything a choice. One parent gave her daughter so many choices that she had to choose from over a dozen different types of cereal just to get through breakfast! No wonder she routinely missed the school bus! Sometimes children want and need a firm but friendly decision from a parent. At other times, a limited set of choices is appreciated.

Stepfamily Enrichment Activity: Taking Time for Fun

Ever notice that a good salesperson will always invest time developing a positive relationship with you before she tries to sell you anything? She knows that half the job of effectively influencing a person is first developing that relationship. Once the person has been "won over," the

sale is much easier. (Can you imagine a salesperson being autocratic and demanding a sale? "You'll buy this because I'm the salesperson and I said so!") The same is true for parenting and, especially, for stepparenting. The more you can enrich your relationship with your child or stepchild, the more he'll allow you to be an influence in his life. This will prevent many problems and make discipline much easier. For a stepparent, it is essential to build trust, respect, and friendship with stepchildren before participating in their discipline.

We'll present a Stepfamily Enrichment Activity in each chapter. Using these activities and the other skills described in this guide, you can strengthen your family relationships over time. If your child or stepchild is frequently out of control, this may be a way to begin making positive contact. Be creative. Reach out.

Your first Stepfamily Enrichment Activity is a fun one: take time to do something fun with each of your children or stepchildren. It can be as brief as a few minutes or as long as a day. The key is to make it fun and to try making it a regular part of your relationship. In other words, "Every day a little play." For example:

- *Throw a ball or shoot baskets.*

- *Bake a special dessert together.*

- *Play a board game together.*

- *Go on an outing with your stepchild …just the two of you.*

- *Share jokes or funny stories.*

To get the most out of this activity:

- *Find activities you both enjoy. Many have little or no cost.*

- *Ask for suggestions from your stepchild, but offer some of your own.*

- *Keep it fun! Don't use this time for confrontation.*

Marriage Enrichment Activity: "Meet Me at the Oasis."

Your marriage is the foundation of your stepfamily. From the beginning—and that includes from even before you've said your vows—building your relationship carefully and then nurturing it regularly is one of your most important tasks. Here's one simple way to make time for each other daily. Create a comfortable spot in your home that becomes your special couple oasis for alone time. Designate that space as such even if it will have multiple uses. Be sure there are two comfortable chairs and whatever else you both agree upon that gives you pleasure nearby: a special treasure from your honeymoon, a calming painting you both enjoy, or a family photograph. This is your space in which you can come together every day for just a few minutes to reconnect. Decide how much time you want to make as mandatory. Every day, you say? That's why you'll keep the time short. Ten minutes? Fifteen? Agree not to discuss problems or the children unless a crisis takes priority over the two of you simply sitting together to talk—or not to talk and simply hold hands. You may decide to bring a cup of tea or glass of wine to this space. Explain this ritual to your children and tell them why you are doing it, asking them to respect you by not interrupting. You could even ask them to set a timer for you to re-enter the family.

If you make your marriage a priority, you'll still be together for your kids after they leave the nest to make marriages of their own. And you will have given them an excellent model of how to do it!

When you make your remarriage a priority from the start, you're strengthening your couple relationship and modeling something very important to your children. While you treasure them all, your children aren't the most important thing in your lives. Your marriage is second only to your health, safety, and integrity. If you make your marriage a priority, you'll still be together for your kids after they leave the nest to make marriages of their own. And you will have given them an excellent model of how to do it!

Family Meeting: Choosing a Fun Family Activity

One of the best ways to prepare your children for success in a democratic society and, at the same time, build the unity of your stepfamily is to teach them the "give and take" that comes with cooperative problem solving or decision making. One excellent way to do this is through family meetings. In each chapter of this guide, we'll suggest a different topic for such a meeting. This week we recommend that you hold a brief family meeting to decide what fun activity your family will choose for this week. Keep the meeting informal and brief, so that nobody comes to resent required attendance. Start by asking if everyone will agree to follow one basic ground rule:

We'll treat each other respectfully.

Next, ask everyone to contribute some ideas about what that means to them, and discuss examples like these:

We'll listen while someone else is speaking.

We'll wait until the speaker is finished before speaking ourselves.

We won't insult or put down anybody else's ideas.

By getting agreement for these basic ground rules now, you'll have a basis for handling disrespectful behavior if it should occur. All you need say is, "Remember our agreement to act respectfully during our meetings?" If this reminder is not enough, you can add the specific violation. For example, "We agreed not to talk when someone else is talking." You may also want to post the ground rules where all family members can review them.

Be careful not to turn the meeting into one of confrontation. Your goal is to establish family meetings as enjoyable times that allow children to have their voices heard and their wishes considered. Stay upbeat and encouraging as much as possible and you will find that family meetings are a great benefit to parents and children alike. Keep your meetings short and end them with a fun family activity or treat.

Summing It Up

- Active Parenting in your stepfamily helps you excel as parents and improves family interactions

- Stepfamilies face three main challenges: Healing from loss, forming realistic expectations, and adapting to change.

- The authoritative (active) parenting style is more effective than the autocratic (dictator) or permissive (doormat) styles.

- Teach children respect by treating them respectfully. Accept that respect must be earned over time.

- Allow children to participate in decisions that affect them to the level of their age and ability: give choices, not orders.

- Agree that building a strong marriage relationship is the first priority in your stepfamily.

Home Activities

The best way to learn any new skill—from riding a bike, to learning how to use a computer, to new parenting techniques—is to practice, practice, practice. And the more you practice, the more positive the outcome.

At the end of each chapter, you'll find a list of home activities which will help you practice the ideas and skills in the chapter. During the next week, make an effort to put these ideas to work and record your experiences on the guide sheets at the end of this book as indicated. The Home Activities will include that chapter's Stepfamily Enrichment Activity, Marriage Enrichment Activity, and Family Meeting. Please make a point of doing these activities each week, and you'll be amazed at the results you begin to see.

Chapter **1**

HOME ACTIVITIES

- Explore the emotional baggage that you and your partner may be carrying. Complete the guide sheet on page 30.

- Practice giving your kids choices and complete the guide sheet on page 32.

- For your Stepfamily Enrichment Activity, take a little time for fun with your kids and stepkids every day this week. Even five minutes can make a difference! Do the guide sheet on page 33.

- For your Marriage Enrichment Activity, create a special "oasis" and spend a short time there alone with your partner every day.

- Have a Family Meeting to plan some fun activities for your stepfamily to do together as part of your effort to add a little play to every day.

Emotional Baggage

Take a look at these examples of emotional baggage and answer the following questions as honestly as you can without putting either yourself or your partner down. Discuss together and be supportive and encouraging.

Emotional Baggage Examples

Guilt	Child's Insecurities	Struggles with Infidelity
Anger	Child's Resentment	Porn Addiction
Resentment	Need for Control	Fear of Being Left
Denial	Overly Critical	Alcoholism
Permissive Parenting	Hostile Divorce Leftovers	Codependence
Autocratic Parenting	Conflict Avoider	Perfectionism

1. The major pieces of emotional baggage that I brought to our marriage are:

_____

_____

_____

2. The one that causes the most conflict in our stepfamily is: _____

Because _____

_____

3. I've noticed that these "pieces" are similar to problems with previous marriages in these ways:

_____

_____

_____

4. The bags that are linked to my childhood and my family of origin are:

_____

5. The bag I'd like to drop the most is: _____

Expectations Video Practice

Scene	Child's Feeling	Parent's Response
Jenny and Li		
Matthew and Sherry		
Javier and Roberto		
Christina and Carolina		
Justin and Paul		
Austin and Tim		

This guide sheet refers to the Active Parenting for Stepfamilies *discussion program. If you are using this Parent's Guide independently and are interested in participating in a discussion group, check out the Parent tab at our website for a group being held near you.*
www.activeparenting.com

The Method of Choice

Choices I can give my child/stepchild this week:

Child's name:

Choice Given:

How did it go?

Child's name:

Choice Given:

How did it go?

Child's name:

Choice Given:

How did it go?

Child's name:

Choice Given:

How did it go?

Stepfamily Enrichment Activity

Taking Time for Fun

Remember when . . .

Remember something fun you enjoyed doing as a child with one of your parents. Close your eyes for a moment and visualize the pleasant experience.

What was the fun activity you and your parent shared? _____

_____

How did you feel about your parent at that moment? _____

_____

How did you feel about yourself? _____

_____

Have a family meeting to decide how you will take time for fun within the next week. Record what you decide. _____

_____

_____

Progress Chart

As you take time for fun with each of your children and stepchildren, record the experience below:

Child's name _____   What did you do? _____

_____

How did it go? _____

_____

Child's name _____   What did you do? _____

_____

How did it go? _____

_____

Child's name _____   What did you do? _____

_____

How did it go? _____

_____

Chapter **2**
Finding Your Way: Stepfamily Communication & Problem-solving

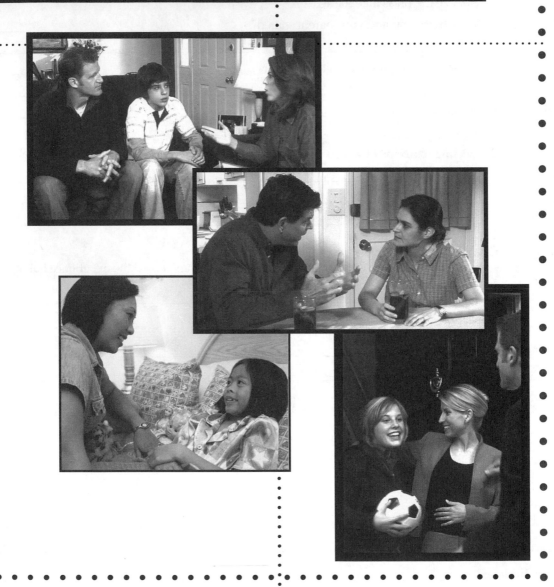

Yikes! I'm a new stepparent! What do I do now? What role should I play with these children? How involved should I become? Will they like me if...? What if I don't...? How will their other parent feel?

You probably have many questions about your place in your new stepfamily—whether you're a stepparent or a biological parent. That's a good thing, especially if you've never been a parent before, because you have to work out your role as you go, and asking questions is a great way to begin.

The best advice we give new parents in stepfamilies is to cultivate your patience and your flexibility. You'll need these skills as you walk the fine line between bringing new ideas into the family and respecting the customs and traditions that the family has already established. Inevitably, this merger of two families with different histories, values, and ways of doing things will be confusing. It will take time—perhaps a long time—to get life stabilized in your stepfamily and to create a real sense of unity and cooperation.

Being an active parent in a stepfamily takes on a different meaning when it focuses more on the nurturing aspect of parenting. This chapter explores that new meaning. We'll show you ways to nurture the children in your stepfamily, and we'll examine effective roles to assume as a stepparent. Later in this chapter, we'll present communication skills you'll need to negotiate the confusion and conflict that comes with the merging of families. These skills will help you nurture your children and give you tools to help them solve the problems that they may face in stepfamily life as well as many of the problems that all children face. Your abilities to communicate effectively and problem solve are integral parts of building a successful stepfamily.

Effective Roles for Stepparents

Ask most stepchildren, especially teenagers, how they feel about wanting or having a stepparent in their lives and they'll tell you plenty:

> *"Two parents are enough, thank you very much."*

> *"I don't need some outsider telling me what to do."*

> *"I wish my parents were back together."*

Comments like these can hurt, but it may help for you to know that they are rarely about you as a person; rather, they usually reflect the child's sadness and anger about how his family has changed. Be careful not to personalize such statements. That's a hard thing to do when a child's verbal jabs are directed at you because it *feels* like a personal attack.

So, how do you develop cooperative and caring relationships with your stepchildren when often they act like they don't want you there? Some even seem to work hard at making you feel *un*welcome—especially if you've moved into "their" territory where they once lived with both of their biological parents. Or, if they've lived a long time in a strong single-parent family, they may resent a new person coming into their comfortable lives and take that out on the new stepparent. What most stepchildren are really doing during this time is testing you and their biological parent's new couple relationship. Just like you, they have a lot of unanswered questions: *Is this new person going to stay? Will this marriage work? Should I bother learning to trust this person? Will I always come in second place—after his "real" kids?* Often children won't develop a relationship or get close to you until they think you'll stay, especially if they've experienced several people in their lives who left. With a growing distrust of their parent's choices, these children may treat a new stepparent coldly, or they might seem fickle: warm one moment and cold the next. Again, try not to take it personally.

Often children won't develop a relationship or get close to you until they think you'll stay, especially if they've experienced several people in their lives who left.

Five Guidelines for Active Stepparents

There are lots of ways to build better relationships with your stepchildren and to establish a positive, effective role for yourself in the stepfamily. Few rules are "set in stone," but do keep these guidelines in mind:

- *Avoid trying to replace the biological parent.*

- *Acknowledge that this is a new and challenging situation for you.*

- *Explore realistic expectations—the children's and your own.*

- *Accept that "instant love" is a myth. Instead, work towards mutual respect.*

- *Work out your stepparent role gradually. Be patient and flexible.*

Avoid trying to replace the biological parent. Your stepchildren have a biological parent somewhere else! Recognize that reality even if that person is an absentee parent or an inconsistent parent with poor parenting skills, a sketchy visitation record, in prison, or dead. Regardless of the circumstances, this parent is a permanent and central fixture in the child's mind. The biological parent-child bond is powerful, and very few things are strong enough to break it. Because part of a child's identity comes from that other biological parent, bad-mouthing that person—regardless of the truth in your words—can backfire and damage your fragile new relationship with your stepchild. Besides, most of what you know about that person you've most likely learned from your partner, and that person may be biased, still angry, or inaccurate.

The biological parent-child bond is powerful, and very few things are strong enough to break it.

The plot thickens when a biological parent is an absentee, meaning that the parent has not been part of the child's life. At times, it seems simpler without that extra adult in the picture and without stepchildren having to move between two households. That may be true for the adults, but it's not for the children. The psychological presence of that absentee parent is always in the back of a child's mind. *Why did my dad leave me? What's wrong with me?* When parents of a young child divorce, often the child cannot understand that the divorce was not about her; rather, it was about the parents' relationship with each other. Similarly, when a parent chooses not to be present in a child's life, the child might interpret the absence as being her fault. Feelings of guilt and other strong emotions are sure to follow, raising many unanswerable questions: *Does he love me? Does she ever think of me? Why doesn't he call or write? Will I be able to see her some day?* The child holds all these worries inside. A stepparent should be supportive of stepchildren who live with such concerns—even if the children don't voice them. Providing this emotional support is one way that a new stepparent can start the nurturing process.

Providing this emotional support is one way that a new stepparent can start the nurturing process.

Whether your stepchild's biological parent is an absentee or just living in a different home, it's important that you begin building a cooperative relationship by acknowledging your stepchild's possibly painful feelings about her parent and promising yourself to never say negative things about that parent—no matter how well-deserved or accurate they may seem. Negative talk about her parent would strike at your stepchild's self-esteem, weaken your trustworthiness in her eyes, and undermine your attempts to foster a warm relationship.

As you help your stepchild get in touch with feelings about her biological parent without passing negative judgments on the parent, you'll reinforce her belief that what she's feeling matters, and trust will begin to grow. Your stepchild will realize that you care about her, and she'll begin to think of you as a safe and kind person.

Acknowledge that this is a new and challenging situation for you. What might it be like for your stepchild to hear this from you?

> *"You know, I've never been a stepparent before, and you've never been a stepchild, so let's figure how we can do this together—and do it well."*

Most of the time, research shows, stepchildren say they just want their stepparents to be their friends. Being *friendly* with your stepchild is, indeed, a good place to start. But keep in mind that friendship between a child and an adult—especially a parent figure—is not the same as friendship between two children. But it's important to understand your stepchild's needs, so if the child needs to think of you as a friend, be willing to explore that role. Ask the child what it means to him to be his friend. Focus on the positive: get him to describe concrete behaviors of what he wants from you, rather than what he doesn't want. Listen. Let him be your teacher. If he says things that you know are inappropriate or that you can't do, say so.

> *"When I hear you say you don't want me to dole out chores or ever tell you what to do, I think you don't realize that I'm your dad's partner now."*

> *"Part of my job is to help you grow up successfully. There are times I'll have to give you directions and responsibilities. I won't make a promise I can't keep, but you can always tell me if you're not happy with something I've asked you to do, and we can discuss it."*

Simply admitting to your stepchild that you're not an expert in stepparenting can take you a long way towards a trusting relationship.

Being a friend to your stepchild means listening, discussing problems, sharing stories, and showing respect. This will help you win your stepchild's trust, respect, and cooperation. But be sure to tell your stepchild in a non-threatening way that your friendship with him is different from that which he shares with his friends at school. You're still his stepparent, after all.

Being a friend is not the only effective role for a stepparent to take. You can step into any number of roles: confidante, role model, mentor, another parent figure. Whether you combine all of these roles to make your own or you try them out one at a time, be sure to acknowledge that this is a learning process for you, too. Simply admitting to your stepchild that you're not an expert in stepparenting can take you a long way towards a trusting relationship.

Explore realistic expectations— the children's and your own. Unrealistic expectations are a big troublemaker for stepfamilies. Here are some common examples:

> *A stepfather expects his wife to side with him in most stepchild conflicts.*

> *A stepmother expects her stepchild to call her "Mom" and to kiss her good night.*

> *All stepfamily members expect their new stepfamily to quickly feel like a "normal" family.*

As mentioned in Chapter 1, now is the time to discuss with your spouse what you expect of one another, if you didn't do so prior to forming a stepfamily. Refer to the chart on page 13 in Chapter 1 for examples of how to use realistic expectations to create positive outcomes in your daily stepfamily life. Defining expectations between you and your children and stepchildren is a challenge best addressed early, as well. Consider it another chance to nurture relationships both new and old. For example, if your new stepchild comes up with a negative expectation like, *"I don't want you to tell me what to do,"* then he's opening up an opportunity to talk about his fears, loyalties, and needs.

> *"Wow! That sure is a strong opinion. Did something happen to make you decide that nobody should tell you what to do?"*

> *"It seems like you might be afraid I'll try to replace your mother. Could that be part of what you mean?"*

When you listen to your stepchild's responses and truly hear his feelings and fears, he'll realize that you care about him and his needs. He'll become more responsive.

When you listen to your stepchild's responses and truly hear his feelings and fears, he'll realize that you care about him and his needs. He'll become more responsive.

These discussions should follow the give-and-take model: in addition to hearing the child's expectations, be sure to talk about some expectations that *you* have and discuss why they're important to you. As you share expectations, you'll begin to tune in to each other and adapt the expectations until they become realistic ones that will really work for your family. This will be an ongoing process. Even if you already have a working set of expectations between you and your biological children, because the family has changed, new expectations are most likely necessary. Evaluate your family expectations again after living with them for a while. If they're not working well, fine tune them until they do work.

In many ways, setting clear expectations is like creating objectives for how your new family will interact with one another to meet your goal of becoming a successful stepfamily. You can do this with your spouse, children, and stepchildren separately or in a family meeting where, together, you'll decide on two or three major expectations that all family members need to meet. Here are some examples of expectations you might establish:

We'll treat each other respectfully.

We'll all pitch in with chores.

We'll make time to have fun together at least once a week.

Accept that "instant love" is a myth.

Building a strong relationship involves developing trust, communicating effectively, mutually respecting one another, and having fun together. Most of all, a positive relationship between parent and child or stepparent and stepchild involves expressing affection or perhaps love for each other. But love is not something that happens instantly when a new stepfamily forms. It may exist between biological parent and child, but stepparents beware: "instant love" is a very unrealistic expectation. When you don't feel the same sort of love for your stepchildren as you feel for your biological children, don't despair: this is normal. It takes time for such a complex emotion—first liking, and then loving—to develop. And because love cannot be demanded or legislated, it may *never* develop. Most stepfamily advisors recommend focusing on building mutual acceptance, trust, and respect over many months.

When stepchildren are still grieving the change and loss they've experienced, they may not act very lovable—especially if they're teenagers. Children need to know that whatever else may happen, their parents love them and their new stepparent genuinely respects and cares about them. They need to feel as though they belong in this new, complex family. Methods of expressing love and affection to children can be woven into the fabric of everyday life: a kiss on the cheek, a pat on the back, a tousling of hair, an encouraging grin or supportive words.

Try to express your positive feelings towards the child without saying things you don't feel yet. The words may come awkwardly, but the important thing is how beautiful they sound to children.

While it's important for you to be able to say "I love you" to your biological children, avoid using these powerful words with your stepchildren before you honestly feel them. This mistake can cause confusion and mistrust with the stepchild. Instead, try to express your positive feelings towards the child without saying things you don't feel yet. The words may come awkwardly, but the important thing is how beautiful they sound to children.

Work out your stepparent role gradually. Be patient and flexible. The following story illustrates this point well.

The Lion's Whisker

An African folktale tells of a boy who had lost his mother. Soon his father was remarried to a wonderful woman who reached out to her new stepson with respect and kindness. But the boy still grieved his mother's death and rejected his stepmother's attempts to reach him. He said harsh words to her and defied any authority that she tried to show as mother in the family. She tried everything she could think of to get him to love her, but nothing worked. The more she pushed and prodded, the more cold and defiant he became.

Finally, in desperation, the woman went to see a witch doctor. She told the witch doctor of her resistant stepson and asked her to make a potion that she could give him so that he would like her. The old witch doctor listened to the stepmother's story and then told her that she must bring her a whisker from a furious mountain lion.

The stepmother was shocked by the task she had been given, but she loved her husband and wanted to be a good mother to her stepson, so she set out towards the mountains where the lions lived.

She soon found lion tracks that led to a cave on the side of a mountain. She quietly walked up to the mouth of the cave and took from her a sack some raw meat, placing it on the ground. Then she walked a hundred steps away and hid in the bushes. The mountain lion, smelling some delicious meat, came out of the cave. He looked around for enemies and when he saw none, he devoured his tasty meal.

The woman came back the next day with more meat, which she again left at the mouth of the cave. But this time she only walked fifty feet away and stood in the open. Each day for a week she came back with meat, and each time she stood a little closer to the feasting lion. Eventually the lion ate from her hand while she gently stroked his fur. Finally, she was able to pull a whisker from his chin while he ate.

She returned to the witch doctor with the whisker that she needed to make the love potion that would win the affection of her rebellious son. But instead of making a potion, the wise old healer told her this:"You do not need a potion to win the boy's heart. Instead, you must approach him in the same manner as you did the mountain lion: slowly and patiently."

The stepmother followed the witch doctor's advice and worked hard to get a little bit closer to her stepson every day. By the season's end, the stepson no longer treated his stepmother like a dangerous foe. For the first time, the two saw the possibility of becoming friends and living happily together in their new stepfamily.

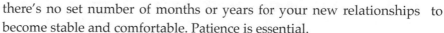

The moral of this folktale is clear: the process of building relationships takes time! Because everyone's pace is different, there's no set number of months or years for your new relationships to become stable and comfortable. Patience is essential.

Flexibility is another key to nurturing bonds between you and your stepchildren. Being rigid about rules and thinking in black and white makes you seem like an enemy. Try thinking of other ways of getting the same task done. Give your stepchildren options. Listen to their suggestions. If something you've agreed upon isn't working well, talk it over and change it to suit both of you—all of you. This is the concept of "freedom within limits" that we discussed in Chapter 1.

• • • • • • • •

When you approach your role with your stepchild from a cooperative stance, you're also modeling skills about caring for others. When you listen deeply, you're teaching empathy. Children know they're being heard. By having give-and-take discussions with them about your expectations of each other, you'll lead them in a lesson about solving problems with negotiation and compromise. And when you bend a little rather than stand firm, you'll teach flexibility. These are lifelong skills that, someday, your stepchildren may recall fondly that you taught them. Down the road, they may even thank you, but don't expect it. That's one of those unrealistic expectations.

The chart on the next page compares two diverse approaches to being a stepparent. Ineffective stepparents often give in to common misconceptions and pitfalls, causing a chain of negative effects. Active stepparents and their partners, on the other hand, work hard to avoid the traps and open the door to stepfamily success.

When Problems Arise

Emma, Sara's new stepsister, went into Sara's room and borrowed a jacket without asking permission. While wearing the jacket, she left a leaky pen in the pocket and stained it badly. Sara was furious about the intrusion and about the damaged jacket. She yelled at Emma, "You're always in my room without being invited, and I'm tired of it. Now you've ruined one of my favorite jackets. Get out of my sight!" It hadn't seemed like a big deal to Emma when she took the jacket because, in her old family, everyone had felt free to use each other's belongings and to move in and out of their rooms. Access to a sibling's closet or CD collection was considered a bonus of having brothers and sisters! But in Sara's family, everyone had a strong respect for privacy, space, and personal belongings. Although siblings often shared their possessions, they asked first and the borrower was expected to return the item in the same condition—or else replace it with a new one. When Emma's and Sara's new stepfamily formed, because there was no discussion about these important issues, each family group just continued to do things "their" way. Often, they clashed.

• • • • • • • •

Ineffective Stepparent	Active Stepparent
Goal is not to be a "wicked stepparent"	**Has courage to be imperfect**
Avoids mistakes by not getting involved	Rejects fairytales and media myths
Needs to be perfect	Knows that people learn from mistakes
Keeps uncomfortable feelings inside	Admits own mistakes to give stepchildren permission to be imperfect
Demands "instant love"	**Is patient, allowing time for relationships to grow**
Expects stepchildren to be affectionate immediately	Sees small successes as progress
Expects to care intensely about stepchildren	Respects and accepts opinions and ways of new family members
Feels like a failure when this doesn't happen quickly	Encourages and nurtures new relationships
Puts down the absent biological parent	**Understands the importance of the other biological parent**
Creates loyalty conflicts	Respects children's need to love both parents
Tries to cut ties with other parent	Guides stepchildren to keep in touch with their other parent
Wants to replace biological parent	Invites the other parent to important events
Feels threatened by biological bond	Views role as being an additional parental figure, never a parent replacement
Focuses on family unity to prove it's working	**Accepts that the existing bond between new partner and his child is powerful**
Dictates activities and directs choices	Knows it's natural to feel closer to biological children
Sees family goal as "togetherness" and "normalcy" at all costs	Keeps jealousy at bay and feels no need to compete
Gets upset when individuals want time apart from the stepfamily	
Resents strong relationship between biological parent and children	
Becomes peacemaker stepparent	**Understands that family life is imperfect**
Sees challenges as failure	Knows that children learn from both positive and negative experiences
Gets defensive when negative feelings emerge	Understands that problems exist in all families
Fears repeated family loss	Encourages full expression of emotions
Denies problems	

*Chart adapted with permission from *Strengthening Your Stepfamily* (Einstein and Albert, Impact Publishers, 2006)

When Peter's new wife complained to him about the hard time she had dealing with discipline as a single parent, he thought his future role was clear, and he felt good knowing how he could be helpful right away as a new stepparent. As an Army officer, he knew very well how to bring order to chaos. Swiftly, he assumed the role of disciplinarian in the new family and laid out a set of strict rules to get his unruly stepchildren in line. But Peter's stepchildren weren't used to this drill-sergeant-style management of their lives, and they wasted little time in rebelling and withdrawing from him.

• • • • • • • • •

As 14-year-old Jim was designing his new web site, his new stepmother came in and stood behind him, making comments about what he should include and what didn't look good. Liz thought that helping her stepson with his project would be a good way to get closer to him. Jim was annoyed at her intrusion but managed to be silent—until Liz said, "I'll bet your own mother couldn't help you on the computer, but I know a lot about this kind of thing." Still, Jim remained quiet, but he felt defensive and angry at Liz for saying negative things about his mother. It hurt his feelings. Liz continued, "Parents of her generation didn't have computers until they were adults, but I've been around them since grade school." Finally, Jim exploded. He threw down the mouse and screamed, "Get out of my space and stop acting like you're better than my mother! She'd at least ask me if I wanted her help before busting into my room like you do."

It's going to take time and a lot of compromising, negotiating, and cooperation to work out a way that feels right for all of you—something that you can call our way.

Each of these scenarios reflects a typical problem you might face in stepfamily life. But each can be resolved with cooperation and communication, and each provides a lesson so that the next time it happens, you and your family can manage the same situation effectively. You've probably encountered more problems in your new stepfamily than you expected. This is normal, not a sign of failure. Perhaps these sorts of problems have you feeling disappointed and a bit overwhelmed. Remember, you're trying to merge two families, each with its own way of doing just about everything, so toss the notion of having an "instant family" right now. It's going to take time and a lot of compromising, negotiating, and cooperation to work out a way that feels right for all of you—something that you can call *our way.*

The Beauty of Problems

One of the realities of life—whether in your stepfamily, at work, or in your community—is that problems will arise. This is true for both successful and unsuccessful people. The difference is that those who succeed in this society are able to handle problems effectively. They find ways to resolve problems, learn from them, and move on. But some people blame, come up with excuses, and make the same mistakes again and again, all the while living in a state of fear and anxiety. Successful people, however, seem to have the *courage* to face problems head on, the *self-esteem* to believe they'll find a solution, the *responsibility* to accept ownership of the problem, the *cooperation* and *mutual respect* to work with others in handling the problem, and the *skills* necessary to find effective solutions.

Where did they learn all of this? Most likely, they learned it in their families just as your children will from you because parents and stepparents are their first teachers. While the word "problem" may create a negative image in most people's minds, active parents and stepparents will view problems as opportunities, for they offer a great resource for teaching your children much of what they need to know and what you want them to know to prepare them for success. The process of problem handling is a way to shape the future—both near and far—of your stepfamily. So, when a problem occurs, as an active parent, take a deep breath and recognize that, in spite of the inconvenience involved, a wonderful teaching opportunity has just emerged.

When a problem occurs, as an active parent, take a deep breath and recognize that, in spite of the inconvenience involved, a wonderful teaching opportunity has just emerged.

To help you take advantage of these teaching times, the remainder of this chapter is organized around the concept of handling problems, especially with clear communication. We'll look at ways to build a cooperative relationship with your children and stepchildren by using effective communication skills. Then we'll examine ways you can help them learn how to work with you to solve the problems they own the responsibility for handling. In later chapters, we'll offer discipline skills that can help you solve problems of misbehavior with your children—one of your greatest stepfamily challenges. Communication is the most essential relationship skill, because it affects every part of our lives. Let's take a look at the "Problem-Handling Model" to get an overview of how this all fits together.

The Problem-Handling Model

The model for handling problems on the next page includes skills presented throughout this guide.

- *It begins with preventing many problems through problem-prevention talks (Chapter 2) and family meetings (Chapters 1-6).*

- *When a problem does occur, determine who owns the problem (Chapter 2).*

- *If the parent or stepparent owns the problem, or if it's shared, use discipline skills (Chapter 4).*

- *If the child owns the problem, or if it's shared, use support and encouragement skills (Chapter 5).*

- *In any of the three cases, you may decide to refer the problem to a family meeting (Chapters 1-6).*

- *Of course, encouragement is always necessary (Chapter 5).*

Who Owns the Problem?

The first step in handling a problem is to determine who owns responsibility for handling it. When a problem is a result of a child's misbehavior, the adults, as leaders in the family, own the responsibility for finding a solution. In these cases, the discipline skills shown on the left side of the Problem-Handling Model can be used to find a solution. However, children encounter many problems in their lives that really aren't their parent's or stepparent's responsibility. The child owns this kind of problem. When that occurs, your job is to offer support using the skills listed on the right side of

THE PROBLEM-HANDLING MODEL

Anticipate and prevent problems through Problem-Prevention Talks and Family Meetings

If a problem does occur, determine who owns the problem:
(adult, child, or both)

Adult-owned

Shared

Child-owned

Provide discipline.

Provide discipline and support.

Provide support.

If appropriate, allow natural consequences to teach.

Let the child handle the problem, but offer support through active communication.

Less Structured Discipline Approaches:
• Polite requests
• "I" messages
• Firm directions

More Structured Discipline Approaches:
• Logical Consequences
• Active problem-solving
• FLAC method

Refer the problem to a Family Meeting

And no matter who owns the problem: encourage, encourage, encourage!

the model. Sometimes, the adults and the child share the problem. In these cases, the adults can offer both support and discipline.

Determining who owns the problem may be a more important part of solving the problem than you might first realize. Children today are very sensitive to their parents trying to run every aspect of their lives and, until stepparents have formed a solid bond with their stepchildren, those children won't take kindly to being told what to do. Allowing children the freedom to make decisions, or even mistakes, when they own a problem is important in building a cooperative relationship. Dictator-style parents take on too many problems as their own. Doormats take on too few. Active parents determine what to do by first asking themselves, *Who owns this problem: my child, my spouse and I, or one of us separately, or my child and we parents together?* In those cases where the problem should be shared, both discipline and support are often needed.

To help determine who owns a problem, ask yourself the following questions:

Who is the problem behavior directly affecting? Whose needs or goals are being blocked, and *what* needs are they? Who is raising the issue or making the complaint? That person usually owns the problem.

Does the problem involve health, safety, or family rules or values? If so, then the problem belongs to the parent.

Is the problem's solution within reasonable limits for your child's age and level of maturity? If not, then again, the parent owns responsibility for handling the problem. As mentioned earlier, here's a case where stepparents who are first-time parents must be aware of what's age appropriate for children.

Let's look at some examples to help clarify this further.

Who Owns the Problem?

Situation	Who Owns the Problem?	Why?
Your stepdaughter borrows your favorite necklace, treats it carelessly, and breaks it.	Stepparent	Accidents happen, but since this affects your property, it's your problem to handle.
Your young stepchild rides her bike onto a busy street.	Biological parent and stepparent	It's the responsibility of the adults in the household to teach their children to use things safely. This is an unsafe situation.
Your daughter doesn't like her stepsister going into her room and using her things without asking permission.	Child	New stepsiblings must learn to work out space and privacy issues together so they can figure out how to best get along.
Your 13-year-old daughter complains that her new stepfather favors his own children over her.	Shared (biological parent, stepparent, and child)	Children have relationships with other adults and must learn how to relate to them on their own. But the powerful bond between biological parent and child may be more than the stepchild can handle, so adults need to help handle the problem so the stepchild doesn't feel left out or unwanted.
Your stepchild has a temper tantrum in the supermarket.	Stepparent	The child's behavior is interfering with your goal of shopping as well as the goals of other shoppers.
Your stepson isn't keeping up with his schoolwork.	Shared (biological parent, stepparent, and child)	The adults' goal of the child being successful in school is blocked, yet school success is also the responsibility of the child. Note: Helping stepchildren with schoolwork is a great way for new stepparents to strengthen the relationship through support and guidance.
Your son is rude to your partner, his new stepfather.	Biological parent	It's a parent's job to teach children the importance of respecting others.
Your 6-year-old complains that he's being picked on by his 11-year-old stepbrother.	Adult and child	Normally, this would be the child's problem, since his goals are being blocked. However, the age difference places this problem too far beyond his maturity level to handle alone.

Notice that some chart scenarios show examples of a shared problem. Although schoolwork is the child's responsibility, adults have a right and a responsibility to become involved when children aren't fulfilling their responsibility. In the case of the older stepbrother picking on his young stepbrother, adult intervention is required to establish appropriate behavior. In these situations, the goal becomes to shift ownership of the problem to the children through both discipline and support methods.

As we move through the next few chapters, you'll learn ways you can support your child or stepchild when she owns the problem. You'll also learn effective discipline skills to use when you own the problem. But first, let's talk about a vitally important factor in developing a foundation for either side of the Problem-Handling Model: communication.

Communication: The Road to Cooperation

Teaching the kids in your stepfamily how to solve problems cooperatively is in everyone's interest. First and foremost, it requires good communication skills. The skills that we'll discuss in this chapter are especially useful in helping the children in your stepfamily handle problems that they own. But you'd be amazed at how many adults need to polish up their communication skills so that they can effectively model positive behaviors for their children. Many adults share that improving their own communication skills for parenting also makes them more effective with coworkers, friends, and spouses. Why? Because communication skills help build cooperation, which we define like this:

> **Cooperation** *is two or more people working together in a mutually supportive way toward a common goal.*

In a high-tech, diverse, and democratic society, children who learn to work cooperatively with others have a far greater chance at success than those who over-emphasize competition. Ironically, although the ability to compete is certainly valuable, it's the ability to cooperate that makes both individuals and communities great.

Cooperation is a product of both attitude and skills. You can help the children in your stepfamily build a cooperative attitude by first developing one in yourself. Show a cooperative attitude through your words and actions by:

Treating your children, your stepchildren, and others respectfully

Enforcing reasonable limits

Encouraging participation through family meetings and enrichment activities

Working together to solve problems

From this foundation, your next step is to develop the skills necessary for working together cooperatively. Without such skills, you'll find the road to cooperation blocked. The remainder of this chapter will focus on those skills, helping you turn your good intentions into positive action and paving the road ahead with clear, supportive communication.

Mixed Messages

Communication involves much more than just what you say to your children. In fact, your message is carried on three separate channels:

1 **Your words**

2 **Your tone of voice**

3 **Your body language, including hand gestures, how close you stand, and facial expressions.**

When you communicate information such as a shopping list, your words carry most of the message. However, with emotionally charged messages such as problems, research has shown that more of the message is carried by body language, followed by tone of voice, and lastly, the words themselves. In other words, *how* you say something is often even more important than *what* you say.

When all three channels of communication carry the same message, you're being *congruent*. That kind of communication is very clear and powerful. However, when you say one thing with your words and something else with your tone and/or body language, you send a mixed message. Mixed messages not only dilute the strength of the message, they also confuse the listener.

For example, imagine that your child owns a problem and you've decided to let her handle it. You say, "I'm not angry. You can do whatever you think is best." However, your tone of voice, crossed arms, and scowl all say, "I'll be angry if you don't do what I think is best." This sort of mixed message makes it difficult for a child to know what she should do. An assertive child will probably hear the message she wants to hear and then do what she wants. Other kids may become anxious and confused about what to do. The key to sending a clear message is to adjust your attitude so that you really accept your child's right to make the decision, even if her choice isn't what you'd prefer. This will reduce your anger, even if you're still somewhat disappointed. You can also change your words to more honestly reflect your feelings.

Example:

"I may be disappointed if you decide not to take your stepsister with you to the playground, but as I said, it's your choice, and I can live with it." (Of course, your face and tone need to communicate this same message.)

Mixed messages also erode cooperation when the adult owns a problem. For example, you're reading a book when your stepson asks if he can stay up another hour to watch television. In a distracted way, without looking up from your book, you say, "I don't think that's a good idea." But your tone and body language say, "I'm not really that concerned, and if you stay up, you probably won't get into trouble."

Whether using discipline or supporting your child in solving a problem she owns, work to keep your three channels of communication consistent.

What do you think the child will do? Like most kids, he'll use the confusion to do what he wants to do. Remember, when you split your message, you weaken your communication. The clearer you are, the more congruent, the more effective you are. Whether using discipline or supporting your child in solving a problem she owns, work to keep your three channels of communication consistent.

Avoiding Communication Blocks

Most parents wish their children would feel freer to come to them with their problems. You want to help them solve these problems and eliminate the pain that such problems can bring. The trouble is that these very problems expose our children's self-esteem like a tender nerve, especially for new stepchildren who don't know how to interact with their stepparents yet. They may be hypersensitive to criticism, negative judgment, and other words or actions that seem to say that they're not worthwhile. Earlier you learned that people use three separate channels—words, tone of voice, and body language—to communicate a message. Now consider that those same three channels can block communication, as well. If you're able to engage your child or stepchild in talking about a problem, you need to guard against anything that might block communication and prompt her to withdraw.

A communication block is any words,
tone of voice, or body language
that influences a person sharing a problem
to end the communication.

Because you communicate your attitude largely through tone of voice and body language, it's not enough just to watch your words. You have to adopt a respectful, non-judgmental attitude if you're really going to help. As a new stepparent, when you listen to your stepchild with an attitude of support, he'll begin to trust you with his feelings and share more of what's going on in his life. The same is true for parents wishing to earn the trust of their biological children, who may withdraw during this trying time. Once you've gained children's trust, the stage is set for you to influence them to make wise decisions. If you jump the gun and block communication, you'll have lost this valuable opportunity to offer guidance and win cooperation.

The mistake parents and stepparents often make is attempting to solve the problem instead of offering sympathy or encouragement.

Study the list of common communication blocks on the next page. Each block ignores the child's thoughts and feelings and instead focuses on the parent's attempt to control the situation. More often than not, these attempts backfire. When people are in pain, they want to know that someone else feels their pain with them. The mistake parents and stepparents often make is attempting to solve the problem instead of offering sympathy or encouragement. Ironically, by trying to solve the child's problems, you may diminish her self-esteem. Your goal should not be to take over and provide a solution or to take away the child's pain; the goal should be to offer a caring ear, support, and encouragement, and to help your child find a useful solution for herself.

The first step in learning to have a helpful discussion with your child or stepchild without blocking communication is to identify your most common communication blocks. Be honest with yourself! Once you are aware that you use them, be on guard the next time your child has a problem, and avoid these pitfalls. When you find yourself using them in the future, catch yourself with a smile—and make a change.

Communication Blocks Chart

BLOCK	EXAMPLE	PARENT'S INTENTION	WHAT IT REALLY SAYS TO THE CHILD
Commanding	"What you should do is..." "Stop complaining!"	To control the situation. To provide quick solutions.	"You don't have the right to decide how to handle your own problems."
Giving Advice	"I've got a really good idea..." "Why don't you..."	To solve the problem for the child.	"You don't have the good sense to come up with your own solutions."
Placating	"It isn't as bad as it seems" "Everything will be okay."	To take away the child's pain; to make him feel better.	"You don't have a right to your feelings. You can't handle discomfort."
Interrogating	"What did you do to make him..."	To get to the bottom of the problem and find out what the child did wrong.	"You must have messed up somewhere."
Distracting	"Let's not worry about that."	To protect the child from the problem by changing the subject.	"I don't think you can stand the discomfort long enough to find a real solution."
Psychologizing	"Do you know why you said that?" "You're just being oversensitive."	To help prevent future problems by analyzing the child's behavior and explaining his motives.	"I know more about you than you know about yourself. Therefore, I'm superior to you."
Being Judgmental	"Why were you doing that in the first place?" "That wasn't a very smart thing to do."	To help the child realize what she did wrong.	"You have poor judgment. You don't make good decisions."
Sarcasm	"Well, I guess that's just about the end of the world."	To show the child how wrong her attitudes or behavior are by making her feel ridiculous.	"You are ridiculous."
Moralizing	"The right thing to do would be..." "You really should..."	To show the child the proper way to deal with the problem.	"I'll choose your values for you."
Being a Know-It-All	"Everybody knows that when something like this happens, you..."	To show the child that he has a resource for handling any problem—you.	"Since I know it all, you must know nothing."

Active Communication

Instead of blocking communication, you can use *active communication*, a set of skills that will help you win cooperation and support your child or stepchild in solving problems. Active communication becomes especially useful when the child owns a problem you'd like to help her solve or when you both share responsibility for a problem. There are five steps:

Step 1   Listen actively.

Step 2   Listen for feelings.

Step 3   Connect feelings to content.

Step 4   Look for alternatives and evaluate consequences.

Step 5   Follow up later.

1. **Listen actively.**
    What do we mean by "active" listening? If you listen fully, you don't just receive information; you're an active participant in the communication process. You listen with your eyes as well as your ears, with your intuition as well as your thinking. With active listening, you're trying to understand not only what the child is saying, but also what he is thinking and feeling. Here's how:

Give full attention. The child may feel encouraged by the attention alone. It says, "I care about you. You matter. I'm here to help."

Keep your own talk to a minimum. When your mouth is open, your ears don't work as well. So listen, and don't talk a lot. Also try to avoid planning what you'll say next while your child is talking. That, too, keeps you from listening fully.

Acknowledge what you're hearing. Let the child know that you're understanding her, that you're truly taking her words to heart. You can say something as simple as "I see" now and then or even "Uh-huh." Ask questions to clarify what the child is saying or to summarize long stories.

2. Listen for feelings.

Most parents and stepparents make the mistake of only listening to the content of the child's story. While getting the facts straight is important, it's even more important to listen to what the child is feeling about her perception of the facts. This will help her acknowledge and accept her feelings rather than keep them bottled up. Some children ignore their painful feelings for so long that they eventually act them out aggressively or suffer from stress-related sickness such as stomachaches or headaches. This is a common response for children during the confusing and uncertain time when their new stepfamily has just been founded. Here's where you, as a sensitive and nurturing stepparent, can help develop a stepchild's emotional intelligence: teach him how to say what he feels and then to reflect on his feelings before deciding on what action to take.

Until your children and stepchildren have been taught to describe their feelings with words, you'll have to listen closely to their tone of voice and watch their faces to discover what they're feeling. Then, name what you think they're feeling. For example, say to yourself:

*"This is a really **scary** situation for Olivia."*

*"Raymond sounds really **angry**."*

*"She's **annoyed** at her stepsister for being so inconsiderate."*

This type of listening is sometimes called "listening with empathy." *Empathy* means sharing another person's feelings. Allow yourself to feel some of what the child is feeling. This helps you connect with her in a way that shows how much you care. It's essential for her to understand that you care if you hope for her to express her painful feelings to you. The result of such empathetic listening is usually an increased willingness on the part of the child to continue sharing.

3. **Connect feelings to content.**

   When you have actively listened to what a child has to say and have an idea of what he's feeling, the next step is to reflect those feelings back to him. You can become what psychologist Haim Ginott calls an "emotional mirror." Just reflect what's there. Reflect the child's feelings and then connect them to what happened—the "content." By responding this way, you communicate the most powerful message of all: you care. Because the content is sometimes obvious, you can often simply respond to the feeling and accomplish the same empathy without sounding like you're repeating what he has just told you.

   Allow yourself to feel some of what the child is feeling. This helps you connect with her in a way that shows how much you care.

   Examples:

   "When your mom doesn't call, you must worry she'll forget you." or

   "You seem a little worried, Jacob."

   "You sound really angry that your stepfather didn't invite you along to the game, Raymond." or

   "I can hear how angry you are."

   "Samantha, you seem annoyed that your stepsister borrows your clothes without asking." or

   "You seem annoyed, Samantha."

   By reflecting feelings in tentative terms ("It sounds as though…" or "I guess…") you don't come across like you're trying to be a mind reader or a know-it-all. If you miss your guess about what your child is feeling, she can correct you. That way you're sure you understand what she's saying and feeling.

Example:

> **Samantha:** *No…it's not that. I just think it would be polite if she'd ask me instead of just taking things."*
>
> **Mother:** *I see. You're more disappointed than annoyed.*

When you adjust to the child's correction, the communication continues to flow, and if you reflect the feeling accurately, an exciting thing happens: the child will nod her head in recognition, maybe say "yes," and then continue to share. She'll feel understood and cared for—and she may understand herself a little better.

Connecting Feelings to Content

What the Child Says	Feeling Word	What the Parent or Stepparent Could Say
"You're not my mother, so I don't have to do what you tell me."	Angry	"You seem angry that I asked you to help me clean the house."
"Dad's late again. Maybe he won't even come at all. Does he even care about me any more?"	Disappointed/Fearful	"Sounds like you're really disappointed about that, even afraid."
"Caitlyn's dad got her 2 CDs when she visited him. She always gets stuff."	Hurt/Jealous	"I'll bet that really hurts your feelings. Do you feel a little jealous?"
"You spend more time with John than with us since you married him."	Fearful	"It sounds like you're afraid that I love you less now and will never have time with you."

4. **Look for alternatives and evaluate consequences.**

   Effective problem solving is a major skill that enables kids to survive and thrive in our fast-changing world. Because most children will immediately rush to try whatever solution pops into their minds first, your job is to slow them down by helping them explore various options and then predict the likely consequences of each. You can guide them by asking such simple questions as:

   "What can you do about that?"

   "What else could you try?"

After each alternative that your child or stepchild comes up with you can help predict the consequences by asking:

> *"What do you think would happen if you did that?"*

It's better for a child to think of alternatives on her own without your prompting. This helps her develop her own problem-solving skills and the persistence to keep thinking of new ways when solutions don't come easily. It also keeps her from being able to blame you if a solution doesn't work out well, which strengthens her sense of responsibility. However, when a child cannot think of a solution herself, you might gently suggest a few. Be careful in these cases not to take over or otherwise seem to be insisting that she do it your way. Remember, she owns the problem, and your role is that of a helpful consultant who makes suggestions but doesn't dictate solutions. You might simply ask, "Would you like to know what others in such a situation have done?"

Remember, she owns the problem, and your role is that of a helpful consultant who makes suggestions but doesn't dictate solutions.

This is also a good time to use the *"palms up" technique.* By actually turning your palms up and saying, "I don't know what you will decide to do, but what if…," you can leave the final decision in your child's hands. This method lowers resistance and actually allows you to be more of an influence in the long run than if you pointed a finger and said, "Here's what you should do…"

Another non-threatening way of introducing an alternative is by sharing your own experiences. Did you have a stepparent? Did you face a similar situation as a child? Include any successful solutions that you found.

Example:

> *"That reminds me of a time when I wasn't invited to a party that I really wanted to go to. My stepsister was invited and I was mad. I sat around feeling hurt for a while, but then I decided that I wasn't going to let the party girl ruin my whole day. So I called a friend of mine from another school and we spent the day together having a great time."*

Be careful not to turn this into a lecture of the "when-I-was-child-I walked-five-miles-through-the-snow" type. Remember, too, that the child is free to use—or not use—your ideas as she thinks best. Unless her solution is unsafe or violates your family values, you should remain accepting, even if she chooses an alternative that you think will fail. After all, she owns the problem. Plus, there's a lot to be learned from failed ideas.

Finally, ask the child what she intends to do, and when. Do this gently, and if she's not ready to commit to a course of action, keep in mind that even great scientists often need time for ideas to incubate before deciding how to proceed.

5. **Follow up later.**

    You and your child or stepchild can gain a tremendous amount of insight to a problem by talking about a solution after it's been tried. Make sure you ask him how he ended up handling the problem and what kind of results he got. This follow-up not only helps your child learn from the experience, but it also validates that your interest was genuine. If the results were good, then a little encouragement is all that is required. However, if the problem persists, or new ones were created, then you can begin the active communication process all over again to find another solution.

    Examples:

    "How did it go with…?"

    "Remember that talk we had about _____ the other day? How did it turn out?"

    "Did you solve that problem with _____ that we talked about last week?"

Putting Active Communication to Work

Look for opportunities to use the five steps of the Active Communication process to help your children and stepchildren solve their own problems. You'll find that the more supportive you are, the more cooperative the child is likely to be. If you're experiencing a lot of friction with your stepchild, however, he may not yet be willing to sit down for a long discussion. You can still listen for his feelings and express your empathy.

Examples:

> *"Boy, you sure look sad."*
>
> *"I guess you're really ticked off."*
>
> *"That must have hurt."*

You can even use this technique when disciplining your child or telling him he can't do something. Just having his feelings recognized and accepted can sometimes make him more receptive and cooperative.

Examples:

> *"I know you're angry that I won't let you stay up later."*
>
> *"I'm sorry my decision feels so bad to you."*
>
> *"If looks could kill, I'd be in big trouble right now."*
>
> *"I can live with you not liking me very much right now, but I don't think I could live with myself if something terrible happened to you."*

Feeling Words

You'll find that the more supportive you are, the more cooperative the child is likely to be.

Although the English language has hundreds of words that describe specific feelings, most people don't use many in their daily vocabulary. As you practice looking for the right "feeling words," you'll find that your feeling word vocabulary increases and the job gets easier. To help with this process, we've included a list of feeling words for you to keep in mind.

Pleasant Feelings		Unpleasant Feelings	
accepted	hopeful	afraid	jealous
adventurous	important	angry	let down
calm	joyful	anxious	lonely
caring	loving	ashamed	overwhelmed
cheerful	peaceful	defeated	rejected
comfortable	playful	disappointed	remorseful
confident	proud	embarrassed	resentful
eager	relieved	frustrated	suspicious
encouraged	secure	guilty	uncomfortable
free	successful	hopeless	unloved
glad	understood	hurt	unsure
happy	wonderful	impatient	worried

Stepfamily Enrichment Activity:
Bedtime Routines and Words of Affection

Children, particularly young children, need a lot of structure in their days. Knowing that certain things happen at certain times and in certain ways offers a sense of security and order to their worlds. As they get older, they can develop their own structures and come to depend on adults less. As with most things, moderation is still a key. A rigid structure that can never vary is just as stressful as a structure that is so flexible that children never know what they can count on.

One of the best structures you can develop for your children is a bedtime routine. Many parents experience conflict and resistance from their children at bedtime, but it doesn't have to be that way. You can use the active style of parenting to turn bedtime into a positive time. Remember to:

1. **Make it a win/win situation for both of you.** You can help make the bedtime routine more acceptable to children if you look for ways to involve them in the process and to make it fun.

2.   **Encourage…encourage…encourage!**

Bedtime can be one of the happiest times of the day for both you and your children if you make it fun and engaging. The following routine has been successful in many families with young children:

Bath time. Begin the evening ritual with a bath (for the child!). You can easily turn a child's bath into a continuation of playtime: just add a little music and some bathtub toys, and make it fun for yourself, too. For example:

"Here's the world famous diver getting ready to do a triple somersault into a tub of wet children."

Teeth brushing. The next item on the agenda, teeth brushing, may never qualify as fun, but getting children involved and using some encouragement can at least keep them on the right track. For example:

"You're doing such a good job. I really like the way you are getting to those teeth hiding way in the back."

Bedtime story. One of kids' and parents' favorite bedtime routines is a bedtime story. Whether you use a book or make up your own story, this offers a pleasant transition from the active play of the day to the quiet of bedtime. One way to encourage a child who is reluctant to read is to choose a longer book, reading one chapter a night. This gives the child something to look forward to each evening. With older children, instead of a story, you might substitute some quiet talk about the events of the day. Whatever you do during this "talk and hug" time, it's an opportunity for winding down and relaxing with a child. For this reason, bedtime is a perfect time for a stepparent to connect with a stepchild.

Special rituals. Then it's time for lights out and your own special rituals. This might include a prayer if you like, and then other regular words or actions—a back rub, a special poem, or something you make up.

Expressing affection. Building a positive relationship with children is an ongoing process that takes steady effort. As we have seen, it involves making arrangements to have fun together, using active communication, and showing mutual respect. Most of all, a positive relationship between a parent and child requires love and affection. All children hunger for these things, even those who make a career of acting "unlovable" and who flaunt a "couldn't care less" attitude.

Kids need to know that whatever else may happen, their parents and stepparents genuinely care about them. Teens, too—even though they may make a show of not needing their families—thrive on reinforcement from their parents. They need to hear that they are a priority for someone. So, parents and stepparents, you need to learn how to show it!

Kids need to know that whatever else may happen, their parents and stepparents genuinely care about them.

Gestures that express love and caring to children can be woven into the fabric of everyday life: a kiss, a pat on the back, a tousling of hair, an arm around the shoulder. But it's equally important to be able to put these positive feelings into words. For biological parents, it's essential to say the words "I love you" to your children, although it may come awkwardly for some parents. Say it every day, and it will become easier. Stepparents, however, should never rush the process and declare love before it exists or before the relationship is ready for it. Instead, take a smaller step and express affection. Here are some ways you can tell a stepchild that you care:

"You're really important to me."

"You matter so much to me."

"Having you in my life makes me happy."

And one day, perhaps you'll be able to tell your stepchild:

"You know, I've really come to love you."

For both parents and stepparents, even if words of love and affection sound strange to you, the important thing is how beautiful they sound to children. Say "I love you" or "You really matter to me" when the child will be surprised at the timing but pleased with the message. Or say it at a time of calmness or tenderness, such as bedtime, when the child can bask in the warmth of the words.

Marriage Enrichment Activity:
Listening with Empathy

The communication skills presented in this chapter will not only make you more effective parents, but when you use them with your partner, they'll also strengthen your marriage. After all, we all want to feel understood by another. We want to know that the person we love "gets us" at a deep-feeling level. However, most people, even in a marriage, have the tendency to only see things (especially problems) from their own perspective. Few make an effort to understand how their partner feels. The result is that each person becomes more and more entrenched in his own perspective and, before you know it, a full-fledged power struggle has emerged in the relationship.

A partner with effective skills as a problem–solver and communicator learns to see with the other's eyes, hear with the other's ears, and feel with the other's heart, without necessarily agreeing or giving in. This empathy creates a feeling of trust and encouragement between partners that opens the doors of communication wide and allows real sharing of solutions to occur.

The following exercise will help you and your partner in two important ways: it will improve your communication skills, and it will encourage you to share important personal information with each other.

A partner with effective skills as a problem–solver and communicator learns to see with the other's eyes, hear with the other's ears, and feel with the other's heart, without necessarily agreeing or giving in.

Imagine your marriage as a 3-legged stool, as you see below. Each of you should draw your own diagram of this stool on a piece of paper. Then, privately, write one thing on each of the three legs that you believe to be absolutely critical to the success of your marriage. If one of these were missing, your marriage would be unstable. There are no rights and wrongs, but do think long and hard before you write. Use a pencil, because you'll probably change your mind more than once.

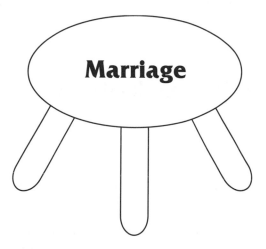

When both of you have completed your stools, share what you've written and why the three traits you chose are so important to you. Talk about those traits—honesty, affection, respect—whatever you choose.

The key to this exercise is that when one of you is sharing, the other is listening—not only to the words, but also to the feelings behind the words. The listener's role is to respond to these feelings, asking questions that might give even more information. For example:

"I can tell how important honesty is to you in marriage. When you talk about how hurt you were when your first partner used drugs and lied to you about it really drives that home. Do you think you might have forgiven him and helped him work through his problem if he had been honest with you?"

Take turns sharing until each of you feel that the other understands your feelings about the three legs. Clarify and question as needed, always being sure to stay non-judgmental and supportive. Remember, no one wants to share his deepest feelings with someone who is going to criticize or disapprove. After you have completed this activity, you may wish to keep the drawing in a place where you and your spouse can see it. Or keep it close at hand so that as time passes, you may want to re-visit this drawing and monitor whether you've stayed on course.

Family Meeting: Talking about Change

Adjusting to change in a stepfamily is one of the key challenges that we discussed in Chapter 1. This week's family meeting is to talk about what some of those changes are and how you are handling them. Introduce the topic by saying something like the following:

> *"One thing about stepfamilies is that they're different. Lots of things change when a parent remarries, and that can be good for everybody, but it can also be stressful. The topic of this family meeting is to talk about some of these changes and how we can handle them effectively together. I also want us to try one other thing. When you're listening to someone else talk, instead of just listening to the words he's saying, see if you can also hear what he's feeling."*

Ask each family member to talk about a way that stepfamily life is different from how life used to be. Contributions can be about everyday incidents, house rules, emotional matters…anything that your family members consider different from life in their former families. You can do this as a discussion, or you may prefer to create a chart (see the example below) as a way to keep everyone on task. Since this discussion will probably involve topics that family members disagree about, you may need to remind the group of the family's ground rule of mutual respect, and

if someone acts disrespectfully during the meeting, simply ask, "Are you being respectful?"

Example:

Name:	*Gloria*
Issue:	*Getting up in the morning*
How we did it in the other house:	*Mom woke us up.*
How we do it here:	*We have to use an alarm clock.*
How I feel:	*Annoyed*
What can I do to help:	*Wake myself up*

Parent: "You really miss having mom wake you up in the morning. I could wake you up, but I think you're old enough to handle that yourself. Is there something else I could do to help you feel better about getting yourself up?

Gloria: "You could buy me a clock radio."

Parent: "I'd be willing to do that. When do you want to go get it?"

Summing It Up

■ Stepfamily relationships take years to build. Be patient.

■ Both biological parents hold a special place in a child's mind.

■ Patience and flexibility are essential when working out your stepparent role.

■ Realize that "instant love" is a myth and an unrealistic expectation. Focus on mutual respect instead.

■ Problems can be excellent learning opportunities. Use them.

■ Determining who owns a problem is the first step to solving it.

■ Communicating a strong and clear message requires that your words, your tone of voice, and your body language all "say" the same thing.

■ Identify the communication blocks that you use, and learn to use the Five Steps of Active Communication instead.

■ Listen actively when your children and your partner speak. Pay attention to the feelings that are expressed.

■ A bedtime routine promotes order in a child's life and can, over time, strengthen a parent/child relationship.

Chapter 2

HOME ACTIVITIES

- Complete the Communication Blocks chart on page 75.

- Practice Active Communication when your child owns the problem, and fill out the guide sheet on page 76.

- For your Stepfamily Enrichment Activity, develop an age-appropriate bedtime routine for one or more of your children. Practice using words of affection or, if appropriate, saying "I love you" to your kids. Complete the guide sheet on page 79.

- For the Marriage Enrichment Activity on empathy, draw and discuss your three-legged stool.

- Have a Family Meeting about change in your stepfamily. You may wish to create a chart to record your family members' responses.

Who Owns the Problem Video Practice

Scene	Who Owns the Problem?	Why?
Katy and Ben (fighting)		
Fran and Erin (broken necklace)		
Sherry and Angela (interrupting)		
_____ _____ _____ (a problem in your family)		

Communication Blocks Activity

We all use communication blocks at one time or another. Or, as one parent put it, "My skill is such that I can use three or four of these blocks at one time!" To catch ourselves before we block communication, it helps to know what our individual pitfalls are.

Think about the communication blocks you tend to use most often. Write them under "block" below. Then indicate the situations that usually bring them out and what you see as your intention for using each block.

Situation	Block	Intention
Example: *Son didn't get the part in the school play.*	*Distracting*	*To make him feel better so I'd feel better.*

Active Communication

After you've had a chance to practice your active communication skills with your children this week, fill out the following evaluation so that you can be sure to learn from the experience.

What was the situation or problem that you talked to your child or stepchild about?_____
_____
_____

How did you approach the child? _____
_____
_____

List examples of the five steps of active communication you were able to use:

1. Listen actively _____
_____

2. Listen for feelings _____
_____

3. Connect feelings to content _____
_____

4. Look for alternatives and evaluate consequences _____
_____

5. Follow up _____
_____

How did your child respond to your efforts? _____
_____

What did you like about how you handled the process?_____
_____

What would you do differently next time? _____
_____

Active Communication Activity

Use this script to identify the steps of Active Communication that Li uses with Jenny.

Li: Hi, Jenny. How's it going?

Jenny: Okay.

Li: You seem kind of down in the dumps.

Jenny: It's okay.

Li: I see. It's kind of tough being the new kid in the neighborhood.

Jenny: Yeah.

Li: Well, I was wondering if you'd like to invite some of the kids over for a while. I could make some lemonade and….

Jenny: Nah. I'd rather just play alone.

Li: You do sound sad, Jenny.

Jenny: Well, I just don't think the other kids like me.

Li: It's tough making friends sometimes.

Jenny: Yeah. I asked Robert if he wanted to come over and play sometime and he said he didn't play with dorks.

Li: Ouch. That must have hurt.

Jenny: Yeah.

Li: Kids sometimes say mean things to each other.

Jenny: Yeah…Do grownups?

Li: Sometimes they do, too. But the smart ones learn that it doesn't pay off to talk mean to people. In fact, I started to make a new friend today myself.

Jenny: Really? Who?

Li: Her name is Laura, and she has a daughter in the other first grade at the school…Emily I think is her name.

Jenny: I don't know her.

Li: We could fix that. I'm supposed to meet with her Saturday to work on the Book Fair. Why don't you come along and get to know Emily…if Laura says it's okay.

Jenny: You'll be there too?

Li: Sure. How about it?

Jenny: Okay, I guess.

Li: Great. Now let's go in and get ready for dinner.

Jenny: Is Emily nice?

Li: I think so. In fact, I think you and Emily will get along just fine.

This guide sheet refers to the Active Parenting for Stepfamilies *discussion program. If you are using this Parent's Guide independently and are interested in participating in a discussion group, check out the Parent tab at our website for a group being held near you.*
www.activeparenting.com

Responding to Feelings Video Practice

Scene	Child's Feeling	Parent's Response
Jenny and Li		
Matthew and Sherry		
Javier and Roberto		
Christina and Carolina		
Justin and Paul		
Austin and Tim		

This guide sheet refers to the Active Parenting for Stepfamilies *discussion program. If you are using this Parent's Guide independently and are interested in participating in a discussion group, check out the Parent tab at our website for a group being held near you.*
www.activeparenting.com

Stepfamily Enrichment Activity

Bedtime Routines and Words of Affection

Family Meeting: Determine a Bedtime Routine

Hold a family meeting to determine a bedtime routine for each child. Be sure to cover the following:

What time is "lights out" for each child? _____

_____

What is the routine? (i.e. bath, pajamas, brush teeth, read a story, etc.) _____

_____

What happens if the routine is broken? _____

_____

Expressing Affection at Home

Recall a time when an adult in your life expressed love or affection to you. Maybe it was a parent, a step-parent, a grandparent, another relative, or a teacher. Maybe the expression was through words, maybe through an action like a pat on the back.

Describe the experience: _____

_____

How did you feel? _____

_____

To help you remember to show affection to your children and stepchildren, fill in this chart:

Child	Your Expression	Your Child's Response

Chapter 3

A Tale of Two Histories:
Turning Differences into Opportunities

Amy Lemon's third-grade teacher knew that Amy's mother was getting remarried to a man named Robert Green, so the teacher was alert for signs that Amy might be having trouble adjusting to her new life with a stepfather and two stepsisters. But when Amy started writing "Amy Lime," on her school papers, the teacher didn't know what to make of it. He took Amy aside after class and asked her why she was using this new name. Amy replied with a shrug, "Well, a Green Lemon is a Lime, isn't it?"

This is a true story, and it's a good illustration of how confusing the transition to stepfamily life can be for a child. Amy's approach to forming her new family identity is unusual, but it goes to show that complex problems—such as those that occur when trying to blend two families into one—call for creative solutions.

In a typical new stepfamily, dozens of issues require the Amy Lime approach to problem solving. Remember, you're not just moving two families into the same house; you're working toward merging two sets of values, attitudes, beliefs, habits, and ways of doing just about everything. That's not easy. As the following story illustrates, the merger process may produce confusion, conflict, hard feelings and, sometimes, humorous outcomes.

Theo Miller and Wendy Matheson's marriage ceremony took place in early December, and the Miller-Matheson stepfamily was born. After a brief honeymoon, the newlyweds had barely moved themselves and their respective children into their new house when the holiday season was upon them. In an effort to create a new holiday tradition (a wise step), the family made an adventure of going to a tree farm where they could select and chop down the tree of their choice. After the involved task of gathering the children from multiple households, they made the long drive into the country to choose their tree. Then the challenge began! The Miller family wanted a tall, short-bristled fir; the Mathesons were accustomed to having a long-bristled pine for their holiday tree. Neither side would back down. After a heated discussion, they finally agreed to flip a coin to determine this year's tree and to get the other kind of tree the next year.

That was only the beginning. That evening, family members found they held vastly different ideas of how a Christmas tree should be decorated. The Miller family liked elegant ribbons, matching colored balls, and tiny white twinkle lights; the Matheson family had always decorated their tree in the old-fashioned style—freshly strung popcorn and cranberry garlands, paper chains, and large light bulbs like their grandparents used. When they couldn't agree what to put on the tree, they began to argue. What had begun as a joyful stepfamily event broke down into a battle over whose way was "right," and the tree didn't get decorated that night, nor for a few days afterwards. At a time when everyone wanted to be in the holiday spirit, instead they felt tense and irritated with one another.

Because Theo and Wendy had gotten married so far into the holiday season, their wedding, the move, and all the other transitions had happened so fast that they'd never considered how having different holiday traditions would impact their new stepfamily. Fortunately, one of the children came up with an idea a few days later. The next weekend, when the rest of the children came over, they divided the tree down the middle, and the Millers and Mathesons stood on opposite sides of the tree and decorated it the way they were used to. Needless to say, they ended up with a most unusual looking Christmas tree. Since the new family needed a solution for future Christmases, they shopped together at the post-holiday sales, and each family member selected two ornaments. They also had a family activity time when everyone made new decorations. And, of course, they took plenty of photos of each other by their bizarre tree for a new stepfamily scrapbook to remind them of their first big family challenge and the creative solution they'd devised together.

Avoid Labeling Right or Wrong

The clashing of values in the above scenario could have ruined the holiday season for the Miller-Matheson family. When the stepfamily was faced with two different, and equally valid, ideas about how a decorated tree should look—along with many other differences of opinion about how to celebrate the holiday—years of experience and emotions with their first families supported their concepts of what was "right." Defending your family's long-term beliefs and traditions as *best* or *right* risks implying that the other family's way is *bad* or *wrong*. To pass such judgment on another family's experiences isn't only unhelpful, but it also hurts feelings and hinders family bonding.

There is no absolute right or wrong way to decorate a Christmas tree, although the Millers and the Mathesons couldn't see it that way at first. The real obstacles for the two families were their different values and their need to avoid change and loss. For any two newly joined families, blending differing values into an acceptable "our" way takes lots of discussion and clear communication to avoid judging one way as wrong, the other right. Active stepfamilies can have fun creating new traditions that will be special to them in the future. Why not consider outside-the-box thinking, like the child who thought of the two-sided Christmas tree as a possible solution?

Sometimes all the situation requires is one person who is willing to introduce the idea of compromise and suggest that change isn't necessarily bad. Will you be that person?

As you merge your families, be prepared for values conflicts to arise on everything from simple daily decisions (which is the "right" cereal brand to buy?) to complex, momentous ones (who pays for college tuition?). Participants in these conflicts usually resist change and defend their ways because those ways reflect their own personal boundaries and define who they are. Resolution depends upon mutually respectful negotiation, compromise, and willingness to think in terms of *ours* rather than *yours* vs. *mine*. When you find yourself in one of these heated discussions, remember that differences will often enrich your stepfamily. Sometimes all the situation requires is one person who is willing to introduce the idea of compromise and suggest that change isn't necessarily bad. Will you be that person?

Name a holiday, and there are as many ways to practice the rituals and traditions that surround it as there are families. Does the Easter Bunny decorate the eggs and hide them, or do family members dye them together? Will you celebrate Kwanza using a the *Kikombe cha umoja* (communal unity cup)? During Hanukkah, are the latkes served with sour cream or applesauce? When you begin to consider the ethnic, religious, and cultural mixes that remarriages can create, working out boundaries and expectations and accepting different values can at first seem like an insurmountable challenge. But approach the same challenge from a "glass half full" perspective, and you might consider it an opportunity for family members to expand their cultural knowledge, learn new traditions, and combine new and old into one way that uniquely fits your stepfamily!

This is also a great time to use the Active Communication skills in Chapter 2. For example, when your family encounters a values conflict, encourage everyone to practice listening with empathy. "I can hear how important that is to you…" is certainly easier for family members to hear than, "I don't see why you have to…" When people feel "felt," they're usually much more open to problem solving.

Sometimes, despite your best attempts to cooperate and compromise, you'll reach an impasse where neither side will budge. In such cases, it's best to adopt a long-range view and choose the solution that is most likely to preserve your marriage without sacrificing either person's integrity.

Limits: What They Are, and Why They Matter

A major type of values conflict your stepfamily will need to negotiate has to do with personal limits. *Limits*—sometimes called *boundaries*—let people know what will and will not be tolerated. They are the rules that define acceptable behavior and your sense of space and identity. They mark where you end and where others start. These "invisible fences" let others know how far they can come into your space or how far you can venture into theirs without causing discomfort. Adults, kids, and families each have developed complex sets of limits by which they're used to living. Some of these will surely clash as you merge families and work towards creating a new set of limits that you all accept.

Limits help to create a safe environment in which children can learn and grow. This is extremely important to children in your stepfamily who are experiencing loss and change. In the midst of so much confusion, they need some certainty, and limits can provide that. A few examples are:

- *How old the children should be before they can stay at home without an adult*

- *Under what circumstances children should call a parent when they are out with friends*

- *That it's not OK for children to talk to adults who they don't know*

- *What is considered an invasion of personal space by a sibling*

It's extremely important for children in your stepfamily to know the new rules, roles, and boundaries for behavior. But don't confuse certainty with inflexibility.

It's extremely important for children in your stepfamily to know the new rules (how we do things here), roles (who's responsible for what), and boundaries for behavior (what behaviors are and aren't acceptable). But don't confuse certainty with inflexibility. Boundaries can be harmful to the family when you fail to adjust them to reasonable requests, such as setting a later curfew for a special event or being willing to bend the rules to accommodate your stepchild's life in his other biological parent's household. Such inflexibility will damage the relationship you're trying to build—especially with teenagers. Likewise, beware of setting limits that relieve your children and stepchildren of responsibility. If you don't give them room to make mistakes, then they'll never learn from them, and they'll miss essential character-building opportunities.

To create new "ours" boundaries in your stepfamily, start by thinking about key issues that are most likely to cause conflict: space, time, money, and authority. Invest time and effort to resolve these potential problem areas, and you can prevent many misunderstandings and arguments among the members of your new family

Space

You can tell a lot about people when you enter their home or personal space. Are they tidy or messy? Do they enjoy reading? Collecting? A specific hobby? When you enter a child's room, you can quickly get a sense of her personality and interests just by observing her possessions and how she arranges them. Because a child's bedroom is such a personal expression, a great way to get to know new stepchildren is to invite them to decorate their new rooms however they wish. You'll learn so much in the process. Their choices may not mesh with your ideas of style and order, but by trusting them with this creative freedom (within limits!), you're sending an important message: *your needs and values are important in this stepfamily.*

A common boundary issue is establishing how family members respect one another's privacy, space, and possessions. Let's say that your side of the family believes in knocking on bedroom doors before entering and asking permission to borrow things. Your partner's side, on the other hand, thinks it's OK to enter without knocking and borrow without asking. These ways had worked in their former families because they had developed an in-family understanding—an expectation—about boundaries. Because that's changed now, the two sides need to come together to clarify new boundaries that define how they deal with these personal issues.

In a home where family members aren't biologically related to one another, it's necessary to set boundaries that define a physical comfort zone.

The space issue that may have the greatest overall impact on your new stepfamily is whether to live in one of your existing homes or leave them both and move into a new one. A new home is often the best solution, but it's not practical for many families. The next best solution is to transform your existing home: paint with new colors; rearrange the furniture or buy new (especially in the couple's bedroom); and make the home "ours" with family photos, art, plants, and other alternatives.

Privacy and sexuality are space issues, too. In a home where family members aren't biologically related to one another, it's necessary to set boundaries that define a physical comfort zone. Sexuality is rarely discussed openly in stepfamilies, but it's important that all family members understand the limits around this issue. In healthy traditional families, the biological incest taboo prohibits inappropriate sexual contact, but this taboo is missing in the stepfamily because some family members lack a biological bond. Sexual attraction between stepparent and stepchild and between stepsiblings is not unusual. Active stepfamily parents will accept this without anxiety or guilt. But it's necessary to set and enforce limits that prohibit *acting* on such attractions and to encourage honest discussion about sexuality. Dress codes need to be established. Require kids to wear robes rather than run around the house in underwear or skimpy night wear. Make sure they close their bedroom doors when getting dressed. Avoid leaving teenagers alone in the house for extended periods of time. Watch for unexplained tension in stepparent-stepchild relationships, as this distancing could be an honest attempt to protect someone from acting on an attraction. These issues can be discussed in family meetings, if age and maturity permits. But since sexuality issues are sensitive and even embarrassing for children and teens to discuss, it's better to have a one-on-one meeting with the child you're concerned about rather than bringing it up in a family meeting.

Time

Do you ever have enough of it? Who gets how much of your time, and when? Time is valuable precisely because it's so limited. As you merge families, you'll probably discover conflicting values about how to manage time. You'll want to balance and prioritize times for work, school, play, and rest in your stepfamily, and because disputes about time will undoubtedly arise, you'll need to develop a plan for resolving them.

A major time issue in stepfamilies is scheduling the children's transition between Mom's house and Dad's house. These transfers can be complex and unpleasant or they can go smoothly, depending on how well divorced parents communicate with each other. If they lack respect or trust, visitations and holidays can turn into occasions that everyone dreads. This is especially likely if a court-mandated visitation schedule is required. The success of these events is often a matter of preparing well and understanding who's responsible for what. As a parent on the "sending" end, you can teach your kids that some of the responsibility is theirs. If they forget something, don't be quick to run it over to them. They need to learn to plan ahead as one of the steps toward managing their lives as young adults.

Help children understand that it's OK to respectfully decline to answer their other parent's questions about what goes on in your household. The simple response, "You'll have to ask Mom about that, Dad," often gets the message across. Teach children the wisdom of sharing their thoughts with others to help manage their disappointments and feelings of frustration in both households. Show them ways to live in two households without feeling loyalty tugs by explaining that both parents love them even though they may not agree on how things are done. Realize that as your children become older, you'll need to become more and more flexible about visitation to accommodate their ever-changing schedules. But also teach them they need to keep both households up to date on their needs and to have realistic expectations about these needs being met. If they return home with negative messages about the other parent, resist the urge to strike back. If the negative message is for somebody else in the family, refuse to act as the messenger. These acts of responsibility will teach children to take care of their own problems without hurting others. Children of divorce learn these lessons early on.

Have faith that allowing some family members to go their separate ways during holidays won't destroy the stepfamily.

During the holidays, when children often have a laundry list of family members to visit and time is at a premium, time management can become almost hopelessly complicated. Before you know it, someone's feelings are hurt because they perceive that visiting time has not been doled out fairly. It's not realistic to expect your new stepfamily to do what your family has always done, so get creative, and make the children's happiness a priority. For example, some children might be happier with their biological grandparents, aunts, uncles, and cousins during holiday times than with step-grandparents, whom they hardly know. Try taking turns. Consider everyone's needs and feelings rather than assuming that you'll all celebrate every holiday together. Have faith that allowing some family members to go their separate ways during holidays won't destroy the stepfamily. On the contrary, attending to individual needs can bolster the trust and mutual respect that you are trying to build. This might sound like a demanding task—hardly what you want to deal with when time is already tight. But holiday scheduling in your stepfamily doesn't have to be a grueling task. Just keep your ears open to listen to the children's needs. Keep the avenues of communication open so that rational discussion remains possible (return to Chapter 2 to re-familiarize yourself with successful communication techniques). And remember the most important thing about holidays: they're about love and unity. Be realistic about which decisions will promote these two premises. Often that means taking many opinions into account and coming up with creative solutions.

Money

Managing money is another tremendous challenge for most stepfamilies—in fact, it's one of the biggest challenges. In *all* families, money is far more than just the stuff that pays the bills. A family's financial arrangements reflect deeper issues of trust, love, and confidence in your marriage. In stepfamilies, managing money and merging values about earning, saving, spending, debts, insurance, and wills can cause many conflicts. At the start, you'll have lots of questions about how money will be handled in your new stepfamily: How much is there? Where does it come from? Where does it go? Who pays for what? One bank account or two?

First things first: every new couple needs to take time together to consider several serious financial issues such as estate planning, wills, inheritances, and possibly prenuptial agreements, so that both of you are fully informed about your financial future. Generally, remarriages involve a slew of additional financial matters: child support, alimony, and divorce settlements, for starters. Leftover financial obligations from previous marriages can complicate getting your stepfamily off on the right foot financially. It might be tempting to avoid involving your new spouse in money matters from your past, especially if you had serious problems. But full disclosure is critical for building a trusting relationship with your new partner. Tell him everything. Even if your past has left you with a mountain of money problems, it's better to discuss these issues honestly now rather than risk the problems coming back to haunt you in the future.

And then there are the myriad less serious, but still pressing, money issues that might seem overwhelming in their sheer numbers at the start of your new stepfamily life. Many of these issues center around your children and stepchildren: sport and club fees, healthcare costs, allowances, clothes, summer camp, gifts, and the "little stuff" that not only tends to add up, but also has the power to strengthen relationships or hurt feelings. If your stepdaughter needs equipment for cheerleading, who will pay for it? Your spouse? You and your spouse together? Your stepdaughter's other biological parent? Often, questions such as this have no precedent; that is, nobody knows the "right" answer now that the family structure has changed. And, like so many problem-solving techniques that we'll discuss in this book, there *is* no single "right" way, but we'll repeat this mandate: discuss money issues with your spouse before they become a problem. Make a list of all expected expenses and decide how the two of you will handle them. After you lay that groundwork, you'll be much more prepared to deal with those unexpected financial demands that will inevitably crop up in the future.

All parents—step or biological—must earn the trust and cooperation of their children in order to gain effective authority, but this is a special challenge for stepparents.

Authority

Before you can establish yourself as one who has the power to make and redefine limits, you need to consider your authority in the family, for as we discussed in Chapter 1, "Leaders get their authority from those they lead." Authority to set limits tells others how much you are to be trusted, how seriously they should heed your directions and advice, and how much you'll let them get away with. If you share your home with both biological children and stepchildren, chances are you have a different amount of authority with each. Or perhaps, if you're just starting out your new stepfamily life, you have no established authority at all with your stepchildren. All parents—step or biological—must earn the trust and cooperation of their children in order to gain effective authority, but this becomes a special challenge for stepparents. Not only is the trust-earning part of the equation more complex, but also you might find that your stepchildren's biological parents want you to play a small part while they take the leading role as family authoritarian. If left untended, unresolved authority issues can turn questions of discipline into a power struggle between parents, stepparents, and children. (We'll discuss stepfamily discipline in Chapter 4 and power struggles in Chapter 5.)

Once you've built trust in the relationship, your partner needs to transfer the authority to discipline to you in the presence of the children.

If you haven't yet developed relationships with your stepchildren, you shouldn't be attempting to discipline them without your partner—not yet. Once you've built trust in the relationship, your partner needs to transfer the authority to discipline to you in the presence of the children. This "transfer ceremony" is one method of establishing a new boundary and clarifying authority in a way that makes its meaning unmistakable to everyone in the family.

If you try to exercise authority over your stepchildren before you've earned it, be prepared for trouble. This is especially true if you lean toward the *autocratic* style of parenting—if you're a dictator type who wants absolute control over your children. Try dominating your new stepchildren with punishments and rewards, and they'll likely withdraw from you or rebel with taunts like, "You're not my dad. I don't have to…"

On the other hand, if you bring a *permissive* parenting style into the stepfamily, you risk losing the ability to earn authority with your stepchildren altogether. Parents who allow their children and stepchildren to "do their own thing" most of the time create added confusion for their stepfamily. This doormat approach to parenting demonstrates little respect for order, routine, and limits for children at the very time you should be trying to clarify and establish those important boundary issues.

The middle road between *autocratic* and *permissive* styles of parenting is, as we discussed in chapter 1, the *authoritative* parent. By definition, such a parent must have authority with her children in order to do her job successfully. By now you are familiar with the principles of authoritative parenting, or what we call *active* parenting: treat children with respect; offer them opportunities to make their own decisions; encourage them to express their thoughts and feelings; balance freedom and limits. Living and parenting by these tenets will put you on the path towards earning authority with your children and stepchildren.

• • • • • • • • •

Negotiating new terms for these four critical boundary issues will reduce future conflict and make living together easier for all. Doing this early in your new stepfamily's history is best, but even later, it will pay big dividends, because when the entire household is on the same page about boundaries of space, time, money, and authority, something wonderful happens: everyone behaves more responsibly. Since establishing limits helps clarify expectations, you and your children will have a more realistic notion of what to expect and how to behave. The understanding can be mapped like this:

That's not to say that children won't test you from time to time, especially if you're a stepparent. The process of establishing boundaries for your stepfamily takes time and the ability to acknowledge what's working and what needs further tweaking.

Caught in the Middle

If you thought you had a hard time adjusting and healing from your divorce or the death of your spouse, try to imagine what it's been like for your children and stepchildren. The primary relationships in their young lives have been torn asunder, the dream of an intact family has been dashed, and they're left wondering how they will fit into their new stepfamily. Part of the job of parents in a stepfamily is to help their children and stepchildren make a healthy transition into their new family. This means building the relationship bonds that form the backbone of the stepfamily while still honoring the relationship bonds that continue to tie the children to their other biological parent.

When conflicts arise, as they inevitably will, it's essential to keep the conflict focused on the two parties involved. It's tempting—and easy—to pull another party into the middle of an argument to gain support. Parents going through a divorce, or even after a divorce, may pull a child into their arguments. But when a child is caught in the middle of adult conflicts, his own anxiety can skyrocket, and loyalty conflicts will surely follow. Sometimes a child will inject herself between two warring parents in a mistaken effort to get them to stop fighting, or even to bring them back together. While she means well, getting caught in the middle usually causes her more damage than benefit, and the child ends up hurt in the process.

Let's look at the relationship bonds between various stepfamily members a little more closely. The sides of the triangle on the next page represent the bonds that exist between members of a stepfamily. Bonds are like glue that holds people together. Each side of the triangle represents an important relationship in a stepfamily. This diagram only deals with one child. We'll name the bonds as follows:

> **Bond #1:** Biological parent-child bond
>
> **Bond #2:** Couple bond
>
> **Bond #3:** Stepparent-stepchild bond

Stepfamily Bonding Triangle[1]

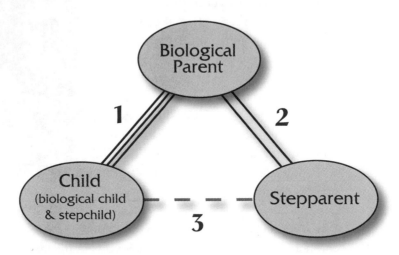

Notice that each side of the triangle consists of one, two, or three lines. Each of these lines represents a bond: (1) a biological connection (family roots), (2) a legal connection (in which legal responsibility is required, not just suggested), and (3) an emotional connection. So, more lines connecting two family members in the diagram indicate a stronger relationship. Relationship #1 between biological parent and child has the strongest bond—three lines—on the diagram. This three-pronged bond reflects history, a legal responsibility, and an emotional relationship strengthened by the other two relationships—a very solid bond likely to hold up under pressure, even if the parent is absent or dead.

Next, your couple bond, represented by bond #2, has two components: emotional and legal. If you're not married, children might not take your relationship seriously because they realize you haven't made that legal commitment. And, if they've experienced several live-in relationships that didn't work out, their trust level may be weak. Kids who have learned

1 The Stepfamily Bonding Triangle was developed by Elizabeth Einstein in an unpublished paper entitled "Understanding Stepfamily Triangles: A Theoretical Perspective" at Syracuse University in 1989. Permission to use or to adapt in any form must be requested in writing.

that adults don't stay around may not bond with a stepparent until they're convinced that this person is here to stay.

With bond #3, the relationship between stepchild and stepparent, the dashed line on the diagram represents a budding emotional bond. But since this bond isn't fully established when a stepfamily forms, a few wrong moves can break it apart. With time and the techniques of building trust and authority that we've discussed, you can strengthen that emotional bond. But still realize, even the strongest emotional bond with your stepchild is never as strong as a bond supported by biological, legal, and emotional connections.

Understanding these bonds is critical because they account for the loyalty conflicts that happen frequently in stepfamily life.

Understanding these bonds is critical because they account for the loyalty conflicts that happen frequently in stepfamily life. For example, a child caught in the middle of a loyalty conflict might test her stepdad by making him choose between her mother and herself. So in this case, the stepdad ends up caught in the middle. If your stepchild is creating the conflict, it's important for you handle it directly, and not threaten, "You just wait until your dad gets home and I tell him that…" Instead, use the skills you're learning in this program to develop a better understanding of what your stepchild is feeling, and begin to work out solutions.

Have you noticed that the stepfamily triangle diagram is somewhat incomplete? After all, the child still has bonds with his other biological parent, too. For that matter, the two biological parents still have a bond as co-parents that must be considered. A second triangle attached to the first would include these additional relationships and look like the diagram on the next page.

Stepfamily Bonding Triangle with Other Parent

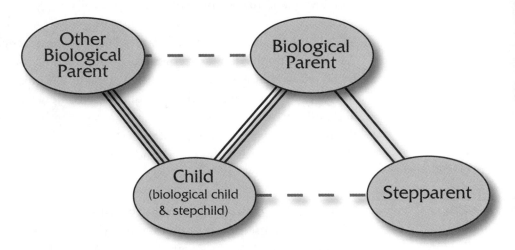

When the two biological parents continue to have moderate to severe conflict, it's easy for the child to get caught in the middle. Active parents will be on guard to prevent that from happening, making sure that their conflicts are handled adult to adult. An insecure stepparent may feel threatened by the strong bond that exists between the other biological parent and the child. Such a stepparent may put her partner in the middle between herself and the child, forcing the biological parent to choose between two people he loves: his partner and his child. Wise stepparents will never force a biological parent into this situation. Not only is it hurtful to the child, but because of the powerful bond between biological parent and child, it can backfire!

As you think about bonds and the loyalty conflicts that create "caught in the middle" scenarios for you, ask yourself these two important questions:

1. *Which of these bonds is the most **powerful**?*

2. *Which of these bonds is the most **important**?*

If you said that bond #2, the marriage bond, is the most important, you're on the right track. Some of you might have identified bond #1—that between the biological parent and child—as the most important. That's the most *powerful* bond. As a biological parent, it's natural to defend bond #1 because of the long and powerful emotional history you share with your children. But to have a successful stepfamily, you must learn to make bond #2, your marriage, the most *important* priority. That doesn't mean that the other bonds aren't important or that you don't love your kids or feel close to your stepchildren. All of the bonds are important! But, as in all families, your marriage must come first. You and your partner are the leaders of the family—the necessary foundation for your family's success. This is very important to understand because balancing the needs and demands of all the relationships on the triangle diagram is one of your critical tasks as active parents in your stepfamily. We won't attempt to fool you into thinking that it's easy—when loyalty conflicts extend to the other household, acting as leaders of your stepfamily can be very difficult. As you try to meet the needs and demands of all your stepfamily relationships, you have to learn to balance time and energy while staying loving and patient. You have to support and strengthen each relationship in the family, and you have to avoid allowing family members, especially children, to get caught in the middle of conflicts. Do this and you will have taken a big step towards building a satisfying stepfamily for everyone.

You and your partner are the leaders of the family—the necessary foundation for your family's success.

Don't Get Caught in the Middle

1. When there's a conflict between you and another family member, either deal with the person directly or address the conflict during a family meeting.

2. Don't ask another family member to take sides in the conflict.

3. During a conflict between others, avoid the tendency to take sides.

4. Avoid putting down, either directly or subtly, the child's other biological parent.

5. Never compare kids with each other or parents with each other.

6. Don't ask your child to deliver disappointing news or messages to the other biological parent.

In the early stages of stepfamily development, when authority, trust, and willingness to cooperate are in constant flux, it's not always clear who in your family is responsible for what. Before you can make sense of this, it's helpful to explore the concept of responsibility. Start by asking…

What is Responsibility?

We hear a lot about responsibility and the need for both children and adults to have it, but what does the word really mean? Let's consider three definitions:

Responsibility means:

1. Accepting your obligations.

2. Doing the right thing as the situation calls for it.

3. Accepting accountability for your actions.

1 Responsibility means: Accepting your obligations

There are times in all of our lives when we'd rather not do some things that we feel obligated to do. These "obligations" are sometimes specifically made between two people. For example, when you tell your stepchild that you'll pick her up after school, you're obligated to be there. Teaching the children in your life that there are times when everyone must sacrifice their own desires for the benefit of someone or something else is teaching them responsibility. Childhood is filled with opportunities to teach this important lesson.

Examples:

- *Owning a pet means feeding it, caring for it, and cleaning up after it.*

- *Being a team member means showing up for practice and games.*

- *Learning a musical instrument means practicing.*

- *Being a student means doing homework and studying.*

- *Being a member of this family means doing your share of chores, following the rules, and attending family meetings.*

Chores: Who's Responsible for What?

Responsibility is a concept; *responsibilities* are tasks. By assigning *responsibilities* to children, parents and stepparents aim to increase the children's understanding of *responsibility*. Before the members of your new stepfamily came together, each of them was probably comfortable with their responsibilities in their former households, especially if it was a single-parent household. Children from one family group might have had very few responsibilities and had grown fond of the resulting freedom; the child from the other family may have been loaded down with responsibilities and made to feel very important. Responsibility levels may have differed radically in your two families, so it's time to talk, talk, and talk and figure out who's responsible for what. In the early stages, it will take several family meetings to work this agenda through so that everyone understands and is comfortable with their new tasks.

Responsibility is a concept; responsibilities are tasks. By assigning responsibilities to children, parents and stepparents aim to increase the children's understanding of responsibility.

Remember "The Brady Bunch"? By having Alice, the live-in housekeeper, always available to do most of the jobs around the house, that TV show neatly sidestepped the inevitable conflict that surrounds undesirable tasks in a stepfamily. It's a phenomenon not reserved only for stepfamilies—most kids hate to do chores—but the nature of the stepfamily makes it especially ripe for conflict over household duties. Battles for parents' loyalty and competition among step-siblings spawn countless opportunities for children to perceive unfairness in the way that chores are doled out. A revolving list of household responsibilities might solve this problem. You should also use disagreements about chores among the children as opportunities to teach about cooperation and compromise.

When you merge two families, you may have children of widely varying ages, which brings new issues into play as you assign responsibilities. A teenager can handle far more responsibility than an 8-year-old. It's important for parents—especially stepparents who have no children of their own—to understand age-appropriate chores and responsibilities. Another thing to look out for is the resistance and resentment younger stepchildren might have toward an older step-sibling being in charge of them while adults are out of the home. Likewise, the one who's left in charge often may resent having to give up his activities to baby-sit the new kid. When you ask older children to do such favors for you, be sure to offer something in return. An incentive will make them feel appreciated rather than taken advantage of. And don't forget the magic words, "thank you." …Or even better: "I appreciate your help with this. It means a lot to me."

Responsibility Between Two Homes

The reality that your children may be moving between two households makes responsibility an even more complex matter. Transitions between the two families can be confusing or chaotic for both children and adults, depending on how clearly they understand each person's responsibilities. Your children now live with two or more sets of rules, values, habits, discipline plans, and ways of relating to others. As they travel between their two households, help them manage their complicated schedules. Rather than giving them fully developed solutions, prompt them with questions and encourage creativity. Do they need to mark days on a calendar? Would it help to have a separate backpack or small suitcase with regular back-and-forth items so they don't have to repack everything weekly?

Transitions are tough on kids. Have you noticed that for a few hours before your children move to the other household, they may be on-edge or appear sad? And when they return, often they're moody and need time alone. Don't be alarmed. Most children experience sadness and loyalty tugs during this emotional transition. It's harder for them when divorced parents don't get along well. It's easy to blame your child's emotional state when they return on the other parent, thinking, "She's always upset when she comes back from visiting her father. What does he do to her over there?" While your stepchild may not have to follow the same routine or schedule that she does in your house, avoid blaming her transition behavior on the other family. Most likely, she's tired or sad and just missing Dad for a while until she integrates back into your household—just as she missed you when she was with her father. Greet her without asking questions the minute she walks in. Tell her that whenever she feels ready to join the family, you'll have a snack ready or some time to play a game. That will give her the freedom to be accountable for her behavior as she adjusts to being back in her other house.

2 Responsibility Means: Doing the right thing as the situation calls for it

Helping your children learn the difference between right and wrong and instilling the desire to do what's right even when it's difficult or painful is one of the more challenging jobs of parenthood. It's even harder to do as a stepparent because you must earn a great deal of trust and authority with stepchildren before they'll respect you as a teacher. But when you begin to see evidence of these lessons working with your children and stepchildren, you'll realize that you've given them a great gift.

Doing the right thing is often a lot like spelling: for every rule there seems to be an exception.

Doing the right thing is often a lot like spelling: for every rule there seems to be an exception.

Examples:

- *Never hurt someone ... unless it's in self-defense.*

- *Never lie ... unless it's a "white lie" to keep from hurting someone's feelings.*

- *Work hard... but avoid becoming a workaholic.*

- *Stand up for your friends and family members... unless they're doing something wrong.*

Taking time to talk with your children about real life situations is the best way to help them grapple with the many nuances of right and wrong. Asking them, "What do you think is the right thing to do?" implies that in your family you strive to know what is right and to do it. When your children do the right thing, be sure to encourage them by acknowledging both the action and the courage it took to act.

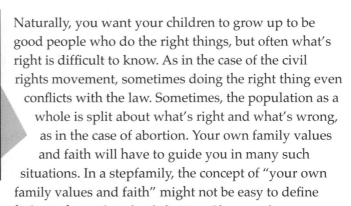

Naturally, you want your children to grow up to be good people who do the right things, but often what's right is difficult to know. As in the case of the civil rights movement, sometimes doing the right thing even conflicts with the law. Sometimes, the population as a whole is split about what's right and what's wrong, as in the case of abortion. Your own family values and faith will have to guide you in many such situations. In a stepfamily, the concept of "your own family values and faith" might not be easy to define or might be in the midst of redefinition. If you and your new partner don't agree about major issues of right and wrong, you risk sending conflicting signals to your children and stepchildren. However, we don't suggest that the two of you learn to think exactly alike for the sake of the children. Like so many aspects of stepfamily living, open discussion is a key, and creative problem solving is another.

3 Responsibility Means: Accepting accountability for your actions

At the very core of responsibility is accepting that what happens to you results from choices and decisions that you make. It's much easier to blame problems on other people or circumstances or to make excuses. But that path prevents them from learning how to make better future decisions. After all, if it wasn't their fault, why should they bother to think about what they could do differently next time?

Early opportunities to practice responsibility and to take ownership of problems help children grow into responsible adults who constantly examine life and find ways to make it go more smoothly.

As they learn to accept responsibility, especially the kind of responsibility required when living between two households, children become creative at solving problems. Children of divorce learn early about the merits of flexibility, and children in stepfamilies learn more than average about compromise and cooperation. Again we see the beauty in problems. Early opportunities to practice responsibility and to take ownership of problems help children grow into responsible adults who constantly examine life and find ways to make it go more smoothly. They have a greater chance of becoming successful adults who, when they do make a mistake, accept the consequences, learn from it, and then move on. Those who never learn this lesson in responsibility often go through life making the same mistakes over and over.

Responsibility ➡ Growth ➡ Success Cycles

Why avoid responsibility if it's such a wonderful thing? Because we're afraid of being blamed or punished for making mistakes. Who would blame or punish us? Perhaps it's critical people with whom we live or work. But even their criticism would be harmless if it were not for the fact that we blame and punish ourselves the most.

Where did we learn this self-criticism? Most of us learned it a long time ago from our parents, many of whom believed in the autocratic or permissive methods of parenting and the blame and criticism that accompanied these styles.

How do we avoid responsibility? We blame others for our mistakes and failures, or we blame circumstances, because it's too painful to accept responsibility and suffer the self-criticism we often heap on ourselves.

We say, "You made me late," or "You made me angry." Or we justify our failings: "Being late isn't such a big deal"; "I have a bad temper"; "I'm a Leo"; "I'm an alcoholic"; "I'm just no good"; "Nobody told me not to."

How can you help prepare children for responsible adulthood? The first step is for you to resist the temptation to blame and punish them for their mistakes and misbehavior. Such ineffective techniques actually influence children to avoid responsibility—to blame and justify, even to lie. Of course, the best way is to model it.

Freedom and the Limits to Freedom

Responsibility requires that a person be held accountable for his choices, but a choice can be made only when there is freedom to choose.

Responsibility requires that a person be held accountable for his choices, but a choice can be made only when there is freedom to choose. When one's not free to choose, the assumption is that someone else has already made the choice for the person. An essential condition for responsibility, therefore, becomes the freedom to choose.

Dictator parents give their children little freedom to make choices. They believe that since children lack experience, parents must make choices for them. Their motivation may be that they want to help their children avoid the pain and pitfalls of poor choices. Stepparents might be motivated by the need to appear helpful and speed along the process of establishing their authority in the stepfamily. But by pushing their own ideas rather than the child's ideas, dictator types stifle their child's ability to handle responsibility. Children eventually rebel against these strict limits and remain inexperienced at making choices on their own. The result may actually be pain and pitfalls even worse than the parent or stepparent sought to avoid.

At the other end of the spectrum, doormat parents allow their children too much freedom to choose. Yet without structure and limits, children don't learn responsibility any better than in an autocratic home with too much structure.

Children clamor for freedom to make their own choices, while parents call for limits to that freedom! This angry dialogue becomes a universal chant, repeated the world over:

"Freedom!" "Limits." "FREEDOM!" "LIMITS!"

Fortunately, a third alternative exists. Active parents and stepparents are acutely aware of their children's need for freedom, but they understand that this need for freedom requires well-defined limits that create a sense of safety and belonging. They work hard to set limits that align with each child's age and level of responsibility. Active parents and stepparents are aware that overly restrictive boundaries lead to sneaking around, lying, and other forms of rebellion; too-loose limits lead to selfish and destructive behavior. Neither is an effective way to raise responsible children.

Freedom within Limits

The concept of "freedom within expanding limits" suggests that a three-year-old will make fewer of her own decisions than a ten-year-old. And the ten-year-old will make fewer decisions than a 17-year-old. In fact, the ideal situation for a teen spending her last year at home is for her to make almost all of her own decisions and to learn from her mistakes while still in the safety of home. As she prepares to leave for college within the year, her parents become almost like consultants. This makes sense when we consider that our goal is to prepare children for independent living, because we won't always be around to provide limits. Stepparents need to understand this. If your own children are young, and if being a stepmother is your first experience with teenagers, it's important to adjust your expectations for that older child. The responsibility level of teenagers is very different from what you're used to. So are the freedoms!

Like most things, teaching responsibility is a gradual process. The lessons involve giving children choices and then allowing them to experience the consequences of those choices. In fact, since responsibility is a matter of accepting the consequences of our choices, then a reasonable formula for teaching responsibility to your children is:

Responsibility = Choice + Consequences

What are your best opportunities for using this formula? First, let your children make more daily decisions. You can allow a younger child's increasing freedom to include such choices as what to eat and what to wear, keeping in mind the child's age and stage of development. (Refer to "The Method of Choice" section in Chapter One.) Second, when you have a problem with your child's behavior, look for opportunities to give her choices and allow her to experience the consequences of her actions. As you'll see in Chapter 4, this combination of choice and consequence is a very effective discipline method.

If you're going to teach responsibility in your family, you have to take responsibility for your own choices, as well.

If you're going to teach responsibility in your family, you have to take responsibility for your own choices, as well. Learn to respond to family interactions without blaming and accusing; rather, listen to all sides and figure out which part of the problem you own. Take responsibility for that part, and encourage others to take responsibility for their part of the problem. This will take you a long way towards avoiding loyalty conflicts and other challenges in your stepfamily.

Stepfamily Enrichment Activities

This week, take your choice between two different Stepfamily Enrichment Activities, both of which address a complication of your children and stepchildren living in two different households.

Stepfamily Enrichment Activity Option 1:
Getting to Know You

Being an active stepparent can be especially challenging when there are two households to consider. Unfortunately, some children of divorce have a parent whose contact with them is inconsistent. Or worse, the parent is totally out of the picture: an absentee. For a stepparent, it may seem easier to just ignore the existence of an absent or ineffective parent, but it's very hard for a child. The "missing parent" is psychologically very important to the child, who often continues to wonder about that absence and may even believe it was his fault. These beliefs, though inaccurate, can erode a child's self-esteem.

If you have a stepchild whose other biological parent is rarely available or absent, watch for safe chances to respectfully learn how this parent is affecting him. Seek to learn things like:

Does he miss this parent?

Does he wonder where that person is and if the parent ever thinks about him?

How does the child feel about this parent's behavior towards him?

What does the child need from this parent?

As a nurturing stepparent, consider opening such a conversation with easy and non-threatening questions. This will probably be easier for you to do than your partner, who may have not completely resolved her feelings about the split. In fact, it's important that you tell your partner of your intent and why. Then try some of these queries with the child:

What are two things you remember about your dad that you really liked?

Do you know the color of your mom's eyes? Her favorite color?

Tell me something funny he did when you were little.

Did she ever sing you a special song? Have a special name for you?

Would you ever like to contact him some day?

As you proceed with this difficult conversation, your stepchild may open up and get emotional. On the other hand, he may clam up or strike out in defense. His responses may be based on what he's been led to believe or has observed other people saying about the parent.

Encourage your stepchild to remember his other parent in a positive light. After all, part of that missing parent may be reflected in the child, and he's probably already heard enough negative things. Most likely, this child needs a credible reason to explain why one of the most important people in his life is absent or scorned by other family members.

If you come up against your stepchild's unwillingness to discuss this tough issue with you, try not to pressure him. Instead, let him know that you'll be available to talk if and when he's ready. Here are some other ways to help your stepchild create an emotional outlet for his feelings about a missing parent, even if he's not quite ready to talk to you about them:

• *Purchase a photo album for your stepchild to reconstruct a snapshot history of the parent. He could ask his grandparents and other extended family members for pictures if his custodial parent no longer has any photographs. If there aren't any photos of this parent, guide the child toward making a scrapbook of items that remind him of his other parent. These could be cut from magazines or drawn by hand and pasted in. Encourage him to write something to go with each picture.*

• *If your stepchild likes to write, give her a blank journal, and give it a title that indicates its purpose (e.g. "Dad and Me"). Encourage the child to write about her missing parent by writing prompts such as "My favorite memory with Dad is…" on a few pages. Assure her that you (and your spouse, her parent) will respect her privacy and not read the journal, and don't ask to read it, either. The point is to provide the child with an outlet to process difficult thoughts and feelings about her missing parent. It should be her choice whether or not to share these thoughts.*

Stepfamily Enrichment Activity Option 2:
Easing Transitions

Transitions between two parental households can be hard on kids emotionally. Different rules, expectations, loyalty conflicts, and powerful emotions can feel confusing or overwhelming. These challenges can also cause adults to make inaccurate judgments about the time their children spend in the other house. Here's an opportunity to nurture your relationships with the children in your stepfamily by helping them make smoother transitions between households. Be careful to assist and suggest without taking on their responsibilities. Of course, first ask them if they want your help!

Start a casual conversation with your child or stepchild like this: "I noticed how stressed you seem before your mom comes to pick you up for the weekend. I wonder if we could talk about some ways I could help you with this." If the child accepts your help, begin by asking some questions like, "What's the hardest part for you: the details, like gathering and packing your stuff, or the emotional part?" Then, listen well.

If the child says that the hard part is the details—remembering what he needs and getting his stuff together—offer some suggestions:

"Would it be helpful for you if I made you a checklist?"

"Would extra socks and underwear in both houses make it easier?"

"Would it help you to have an extra backpack or small suitcase to keep packed with essentials already in it?"

"Would a printout of your activity schedule be useful?"

If the child says it's the emotional part that's the hardest, ask what you can to do make that time easier for him. Would it be more helpful if you made yourself scarce when his mom came to get him? Or would he rather you be present? Let the child know that when he returns, it's fine with you if he goes directly to his room and shuts the door to be alone for some time. Let him know you understand that he needs time to think and readjust. Let him feel your care and compassion without any pressure from you about swiftly integrating back into this part of his family.

Marriage Enrichment Activity: Values Summit

In this chapter we discussed how differing values between family groups can cause conflict in stepfamilies. When each group feels that its values are the right ones (while the other's values are wrong), and neither is willing to compromise, trouble is sure to follow. Your behaviors and decisions, including your ideas about parenting, are rooted in your values. These deep and personal beliefs likely originated with the family that raised you, and they have been shaped by the experiences of your entire lifetime. As you and your partner shape your stepfamily by setting new expectations and deciding what limits you will put in place, your values will come into play. You may find that your values clash with your partner's in ways that make stepfamily planning more difficult. That's "the hard way" to discover your partner's values. To avoid future conflict and deepen the bond you share with your partner, it's a good idea to talk about your values before the time comes to apply them to your stepfamily leadership.

For this Marriage Enrichment Activity, have a "values summit" with your partner. If you and your partner completed the "three legged stool" activity from Chapter 2 that helped you understand what each of you believe about marriage, you'll have a head start on this activity. But this time, start by choosing one of the four boundary issues discussed in this chapter: space (including sexuality), time, money, or authority. First, spend some time thinking by yourself about how your values influence your choices and opinions around this issue. Then, get together with your partner in your "oasis" to share your views. Be open to the idea of your partner having a different perspective.

Your mutual goals should be:

- *to understand a little bit more about your partner's beliefs.*

- *to move closer to the goal of setting limits around _____ (space, time, money, or authority) in a way that reflects both of your values.*

The more you know about your partner's values (and vice versa), the more capable both of you will be of setting clear limits in your stepfamily. Limits that go through this process will be stronger than those set with weak or clashing values underlying them.

Family Meeting: Allowances and Chores

Most of the work required to run a family obviously falls on the parents and stepparents, but it's important to begin teaching children when they're young the value of family work and their responsibilities as family members. Another aspect of responsibility that kids should learn early is how to handle money. Parents can facilitate this lesson by giving children a fixed amount of money each week to spend as they like—an allowance. This should replace the need for kids to nickel and dime their parents for things they want to buy over the course of the week. The parent simply has to remind the child, "That's what your allowance is for."

While some parents like to pay children for doing their chores, we recommend that you avoid this temptation. Paying children for chores interferes with a valuable lesson: in a family, everyone shares the work, and everyone shares the resources. You pitch in because you're part of the family, not because you're getting paid to do it.

In a family, everyone shares the work, and everyone shares the resources. You pitch in because you're part of the family, not because you're getting paid to do it.

If a child fails to do his chores in a timely manner, that's where your discipline skills will come in. See Chapter 4 for an in-depth look at those skills.

A few tips on allowances and chores:

Allowances:

• *Begin giving out allowance when a child can understand and count money, usually around age 6 or 7. Start by giving her a set amount to spend on outings—to buy souvenirs when going to a special event, for example.*

• *Give older kids a weekly allowance that increases with age. Be sure to specify what the allowance is meant to cover: entertainment and personal purchases like music and games, for example. With teens, you might eventually include an allowance for clothing and gas money to help them prepare for independence.*

• *Don't tell your child what he can and can't use his allowance to buy, except in matters of health, safety, and the law. If he wants to "blow" his money on video games, that's his choice. You can use active communication to help him evaluate his decision-making skills and consider other alternatives, but ultimately it's his choice. Even if he makes a poor choice, you must allow him to learn through the experience.*

• *Teach kids the value of saving money by offering to match (at a rate of your choosing) any money that they save. You should decide together what the banked money may be used for later, such as, a new bike.*

Chores:

- *Make a master list of all the chores that must be done to run the family. Include adult-only chores like earning money, driving (until kids have their licenses), cooking, and shopping. This helps the kids appreciate all you do.*

- *Decide which chores each family member will do, keeping the choices age-appropriate. Use negotiation skills to assign chores fairly, or make a work wheel that rotates chores from person to person, but don't simply dictate who does what.*

- *Change chore assignments once a month or more often so that no one gets stuck with a less-desirable chore for too long.*

- *It's okay to give kids extra jobs to earn extra money. For example, washing your car or shining your shoes are chores that might not be on the weekly list, but you'd appreciate a child doing them for you.*

Have a family meeting this week to discuss allowances and chores. Remind everyone of your basic ground rules, especially mutual respect, and use your active communication skills to consider what others are feeling. Make sure someone takes notes so that you have a record of all the chores, allowances, and special agreements that you decide upon at the meeting. As always, end on a positive note: a fun activity or an edible treat, for instance.

Summing It Up

- Clear limits lead to responsible behavior.

- Set boundaries around issues of time, space, money, and authority.

- Transitions between two households are challenging for children.

- Children must learn to be accountable for their behavior and decisions.

- Values, beliefs, and attitudes may differ but shouldn't be viewed as right or wrong.

- The biological parent–child bond is very powerful.

- Loyalty conflicts create "caught in the middle" scenarios that build tension among stepfamily members.

- The marriage relationship is the most important bond in the stepfamily.

- Freedom within limits is essential for children to learn responsibility.

- Allowances and chores help children learn responsibility.

Chapter 3

HOME ACTIVITIES

- Complete the guide sheet about stepfamily limits on page 116.

- Avoid the tendency to get caught in the middle or to put someone else in the middle, and complete the guide sheet on page 117.

- Do the Stepfamily Enrichment Activity that best suits your stepfamily situation: either "Getting to Know You" or "Easing Transitions."

- For your Marriage Enrichment Activity, have a "values summit" to discuss your thoughts and beliefs about space, time, money, or authority in your stepfamily.

- Have a Family Meeting about allowances and chores.

Limits and Boundaries

Think about the limits that you've established in your stepfamily to handle issues of time, space, money, and authority.

1. What limits around **time** issues have you established for the children in your family? These include: curfews; time they spend on TV, video games, Internet, and telephone; time you spend together as a family; homework time, etc. _____

   _____

   _____

2. What areas still need to be addressed? _____

   _____

3. What limits regarding **space** have you established in your family? These have to do with sharing living space, tidiness/messiness, respecting privacy, knocking on doors, etc. _____

   _____

   _____

4. What areas still need to be addressed? _____

   _____

5. What limits have you established in your family regarding **money**? This includes allowances, who pays for what, earning extra money, shared expenses with former spouses, etc. _____

   _____

   _____

6. What areas still need to be addressed? _____

   _____

7. What limits regarding parental **authority** have you established in your family? This includes issues of discipline, decision-making, etc. _____

   _____

   _____

8. What areas still need to be addressed? _____

   _____

Avoid "Caught in the Middle" Situations

This week, think about how you either get caught in the middle or how you pull someone else into the middle, creating loyalty conflicts and stressful feelings. Then, try to catch yourself before you make this mistake again. Answer the following questions.

1. Were you able to handle a conflict with a family member either directly with the person or in a family meeting? Describe what happened. _____

   _____

   _____

   _____

2. Were you tempted to ask other family members to take sides? _____
   Describe what happened. _____

   _____

   _____

3. Did you avoid the tendency to take sides during a conflict between others? _____
   What was the result? _____

   _____

   _____

   _____

4. Did you avoid putting down, either directly or subtly, a child's biological parent? _____
5. Did you avoid comparing kids with each other or parents with each other? _____
6. Did you avoid asking kids to deliver disappointing messages to the other biological parent?
   How did it feel to avoid these behaviors?_____

   _____

   _____

7. Were there any situations in which you got caught in the middle or saw someone else caught?
   If so, describe what happened and the effect it had on you and the other people involved. ___

   _____

   _____

Chapter 4
The Challenge of Discipline

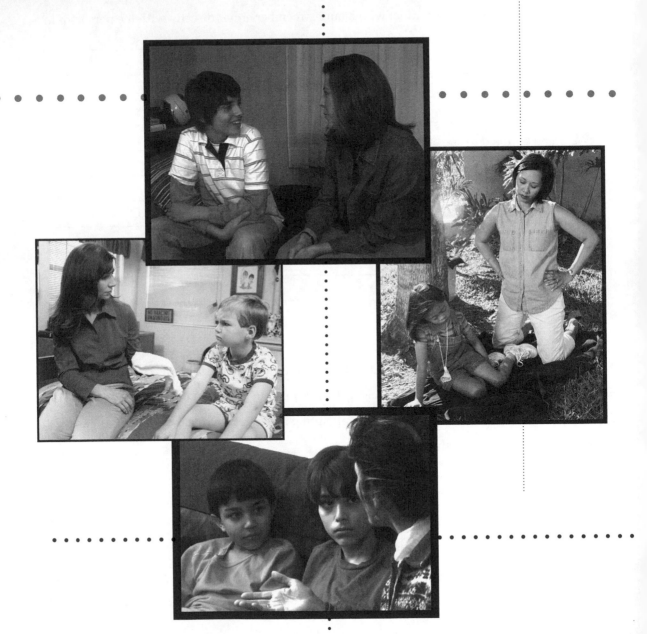

Discipline is one of the most important challenges that stepfamily parents will face, and yet many couples form stepfamilies without any sort of discipline plan. They don't realize that on top of the normal challenge of disciplining children, they'll also need to: merge two families' views and values about discipline into one effective "ours" way; work out who has the authority to discipline whose children; and deal with the complexities of handling discipline when children live in two or more households. In this chapter, we'll discuss the best discipline practices and how to make them work in your stepfamily. But first let's examine why some commonly used discipline techniques no longer work.

Reward and Punishment Often Backfire

Discipline is vital for teaching children how to live within the limits and values of your family and society. The word comes from the Latin *disciplina*, which means "to teach." How you choose to teach the children in your family right from wrong, the importance of fulfilling their obligations, and accepting responsibility for their actions prepares them for leaving the safety of your family.

Effective child discipline doesn't necessarily mean reward and punishment. Earlier we proposed that reward and punishment are ways the dictator parent enforces orders. These parents keep children in line with the threat of punishment if they misbehave and the promise of reward if they follow parents' orders. Interestingly, stepparents without children of their own often assume this dictator role. They may have good intentions—perhaps to help "straighten out those unruly kids" who are accustomed to living with a permissive single parent without routines or limits. But this parenting style often backfires and hinders building trust and friendship with stepchildren. This system of reward and punishment may have been effective in medieval days when peasants were ruled by kings, queens, and emperors, and everyone "knew his place" on the ladder of authority, but in a society of equals and a world where the traditional family structure is no longer the norm, it doesn't work very well.

REWARD:
Something extra that is used to bribe the child to change behavior.

When you reward a child for good behavior, she may come to expect a reward almost as a right. She doesn't learn to behave cooperatively just because the situation calls for it or because the family functions better when everyone follows the rules. Instead, she may develop a "what's in it for me" attitude that leads her to expect more and more rewards for positive behavior. You must then increase the value of the reward to keep your system effective until you reach a point of frustration. This frustration often leads to the use of punishment.

PUNISHMENT:
Something that is used to hurt the child to change behavior.

Punishment may stop kids from misbehaving in the short run, but in the long run, it can cause hurt, resentment, guilt, dishonesty, and anxiety in a child. Often, teenagers—especially teenage stepchildren—will simply rebel rather than accept punishment.

In a society of equals, when you hurt someone, most people feel that the victim has an unspoken right to hurt you back. Children will usually find ways of getting even with punishing parents through future misbehavior. The practice of reward and punishment depends on parents being superior and children inferior, an idea which is out of place in a society based on equality. Instead of supporting the use of rewards and punishment, we'll be exploring how logically connected incentives ("when/then choices") and consequences ("either/or choices") can be used to help motivate positive behavior. These methods imply mutual respect and equality without parents having to give up their authority. Using incentives rather than rewards and punishments will improve your discipline efforts and help you lead your stepfamily toward success.

The Think-Feel-Do Cycle

Effective discipline of children in any family requires some understanding of what motivates them—why children do what they do. Let's consider how four separate aspects of a child's motivation are related: events (something that happens in the child's life); thoughts (including his beliefs, attitudes and values); feelings; and behavior. We call this the "think-feel-do cycle".

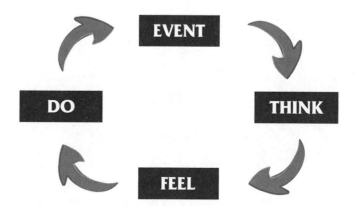

This is how the cycle works: When something happens to a child (an event), he thinks about it, both consciously and unconsciously. All of his attitudes, needs, and values about such situations and about himself come into play. This thinking then produces a feeling. Many people mistakenly believe that feelings just happen, but they are really products of our thoughts and values. Change the thinking and you change the feelings, too. Together, the thinking and feeling produce an action (behavior). As the event changes or remains the same, the child will have new thoughts, feelings, and behavior as the system goes around and around.

Example:

> Ten-year-old Steven's stepmother notices that he has left the milk out on the counter. She says in an angry voice, "Steven, how many times do I have to tell you to put the milk back in the refrigerator?!"

This event triggers a lot of conscious and unconscious thoughts for Steven, including:

> Here goes my stepmother on my case again.
>
> She has no right to yell at me.
>
> She'll never love me like she loves her own kids.
>
> I'm tired of her putting me down all the time.

These thoughts produce feelings of anger and resentment, which then trigger the following actions:

> A scowl
>
> A stiffening of the back

…and the following sharp reply:

> "You're not my mother! I don't have to do what you say!"

This triggers the stepmother's own think-feel-do cycle and the angry response:

> "As long as you live under this roof, you'll live by my rules!"

Stepmom's autocratic style and her punishing remark triggers Steven's rebellious attitude and thoughts of "she can't treat me this way" as he storms out of the room in anger—and the cycle continues.

Parents and stepparents aren't the only events in their children's lives. Every day is filled with many situations to which kids constantly respond with thoughts, feelings, and behavior. The most dangerous of these events could lead to violence and unsafe risks. Later, as children become preteens and teens, events may take the form of offers to use drugs or to engage in sexual activity that violates family values. One of your jobs as parents and stepparents is to filter out as many of these unsafe events as possible. This includes such actions as:

Knowing where kids are and who is supervising them

Knowing who their friends are and encouraging positive friendships

Monitoring and setting limits on their use of media, including the Internet, TV, music, and movies

Keeping them away from unsafe people and places

You'll learn more about parents acting as filters in Chapter 6.

Your ultimate goal should be to teach children the attitudes, values, and self-esteem that will give them the courage and character to make wise decisions when they're faced with challenging events.

However, since you'll not always be there to act as filters, your ultimate goal should be to teach children the attitudes, values, and self-esteem that will give them the courage and character to make wise decisions when they're faced with challenging events. Positive behavior leads to positive results, which increases self-esteem and courage, leading to more positive behavior. This is called a **success cycle**.

Success Cycle

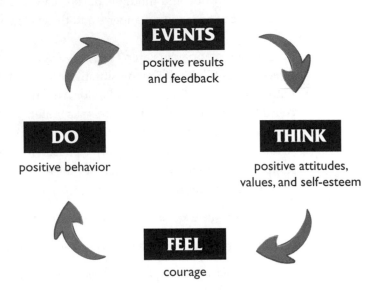

Of course, the opposite can also occur. Negative attitudes, poor values, and low self-esteem can produce discouragement and negative behavior, which leads to poor results and punishment. This lowers self-esteem further, producing more discouragement and negative behavior—causing a "failure cycle." The keys to teaching our children the thinking that produces a success cycle (and breaks a failure cycle) include the following:

- *Treating your children respectfully and encouraging their participation in decisions that affect them (Chapters 1 and 5)*

- *Using effective communication skills to talk about current and potential problems while instilling your family values (Chapter 2)*

- *Using effective discipline techniques to set limits and consequences and to teach responsibility (Chapter 4)*

- *Building self-esteem and courage, and encouraging mutual respect and cooperation (Chapters 1, 2, and 5)*

- *Filtering negative influences, where possible, and talking about how to handle high-risk events (Chapters 5 and 6)*

Stepfamily Considerations

Many of the discipline methods that work for traditional, intact families also work for stepfamilies, but several aspects of stepfamily living make discipline more challenging. Unclear authority to discipline is responsible for much conflict and confusion. It's not always clear whether a parent or stepparent has the authority to discipline. Several factors contribute to this:

1. **Weak stepparent-stepchild bond**: If you're a new stepparent, chances are that you haven't developed mutual respect, trust, and a strong bond of caring with your stepchildren. With your effort, these will develop over time, but before they do, you lack authority to wield discipline.

2. **No united front**: You and your partner may have different parenting styles and different ideas about discipline. When you don't present a "united front" as a parental team, your children might suffer from loyalty conflicts or learn to take advantage of your disagreement in order to get their way.

3. **Resistance to change**: Your biological children are used to your former style of parenting and discipline and probably will resent a new stepparent telling them what to do too soon. Even if the biological parent makes the changes, most kids will blame the stepparent for rocking the boat.

4. **Multiple households = Multiple discipline styles:**
   The style of discipline your children experience in their other household may differ vastly from yours. It's unrealistic to expect that when you apply a consequence for misbehavior in your household, the discipline will be carried over to the other household.

Generally, you cannot control discipline there, and the parents in that household may resent your attempt to do so. Unless you have excellent communication and a very positive relationship with those parents, it's best to let them handle the kids' discipline their own way.

5. **Unclear responsibility:** Children in your stepfamily may be confused about which adult they should listen to when it comes to discipline, especially if the adults haven't agreed upon a common set of rules and consequences. Give a child too many conflicting discipline messages, and she might just decide not to heed any of them.

You must be willing to make your stepfamily success a long-term project that depends on gradual developments.

None of these challenges are permanent conditions in stepfamilies, but until they've been resolved, parents need to adjust their discipline efforts by making changes slowly and discussing each step with the family. You can prevent much conflict by holding family meetings to discuss each of your roles and responsibilities. And remember that patience is essential. You must be willing to make your stepfamily success a long-term project that depends on gradual developments. As a stepparent, one of these gradual developments is your role as a disciplinarian in the family.

Transferring Authority to the Stepparent

We mentioned earlier that a stepparent doesn't have the authority to discipline her stepchildren at the very beginning. As a stepparent, you must first build a bond of trust and respect through nurturing to earn authority with your stepchildren. This might take a long time, but it's important that you not rush the process. When you and your partner agree that your relationship with your stepchildren has grown strong enough for you to take part in discipline, plan a formal transfer of authority. This must be played out in front of the children so that the change is very clear for them. Your partner—your stepchildren's biological parent—needs to be there to transfer the authority to discipline them to you. It might sound like this:

"Kids, Nora and I have been discussing how our stepfamily has changed, and we agree that all of us have to come to trust each other enough now that we're ready for this. When I'm not here and you make a bad decision or break a house rule, Nora has my permission to discipline you. She'll be in charge! Do you have any questions about how that will work?"

This transfer of authority sets the stage for both parents to discipline, but it's only part of the work that's necessary to prepare for effective discipline in your stepfamily. Of course, stepkids will test their stepparents new authority. Biological parents need to be supportive and back up their partner's decisions. If necessary, these decisions can be re-addressed and altered in a private conference between partners. While any two partners can differ in opinion about discipline, those who start a stepfamily together have differences backed by separate family histories—perhaps many years of dealing with discipline "my way." These can be very powerful differences, so you and your partner might have a difficult job ahead of you. Read the following section about effective discipline carefully, considering how the discipline methods we present will work with your newly merged family. The techniques we'll present are a middle road between the approaches used by authoritarian and permissive parents. If you and your partner are looking for an alternative to smooth out the differences enforced by years of "my way" discipline, this is a good place to start.

Effective Discipline

In Chapter 1, we discussed the importance of using problems as teaching tools for instilling qualities of character such as cooperation, courage, and responsibility in children. Let's refer again to the Problem-Handling Model that we presented in that chapter and notice the highlighted areas.

This chart illustrates methods of preventing problems and then shows you how to handle problems that parents and stepparents own, using effective discipline. The rest of this chapter focuses on how to use these powerful skills to teach your child responsibility and how to live within the limits that you determine as the leader in the family.

Of course, you can't prevent all problems. At times your children or stepchildren will become discouraged and turn to negative behavior to achieve their goals. Consider discipline as a motivator for your children to change behavior. When using any of the discipline skills that will follow, keep in mind these tips:

1. **Your goal is to teach your children, not to scare, shame, or hurt them.** In fact, we can teach far better without hurting their feelings or their bodies.

2. **Whenever you discipline a child for negative behavior, be sure to explore the roots of why that misbehavior occurred and find opportunities to encourage any improvement the child makes.**

3. **When using discipline to influence your children, you always want to use the least assertive method that works.**

When your children know that you're disciplining them because you care, it's easier for them to accept.

4. **Let discipline be motivated by caring.** When your children know that you're disciplining them because you care, it's easier for them to accept. When you discipline out of frustration, anger, and your own desires, it's difficult for your child to accept or learn the lesson you're trying to teach.

The first three discipline methods we'll present are basic communication methods that increase in assertiveness from mild to firm. Start with the first, and if it doesn't work, move on to the second and then the third. They are:

- *Polite Requests*

- *"I" Messages*

- *Firm reminders*

THE PROBLEM-HANDLING MODEL

Anticipate and prevent problems through Problem-Prevention Talks and Family Meetings

If a problem does occur, determine who owns the problem:
(adult, child, or both)

Adult-owned	Shared	Child-owned

Provide discipline.   **Provide discipline and support.**   **Provide support.**

Less Structured Discipline Approaches:
- Polite requests
- "I" messages
- Firm directions

More Structured Discipline Approaches:
- Logical Consequences
- Active problem-solving
- FLAC method

If appropriate, allow natural consequences to teach.

Let the child handle the problem, but offer support through active communication.

Refer the problem to a Family Meeting

And no matter who owns the problem: encourage, encourage, encourage!

Polite Requests

Not every problem or conflict requires a full-fledged discussion or firm discipline. As we said before, sometimes the reason children misbehave is simply because they don't know what you expect of them. This is especially common in new stepfamilies, where so many factors contribute to unclear expectations. Often, a polite request is enough to influence a child to change behavior. It's also an excellent way to set new expectations with children and stepchildren.

Take, for example, the following situation:

Your 8-year-old stepson, Daryl, has a habit of leaving dirty dishes in the den, expecting that someone else (i.e. you, his stepmother) will take the dishes to the kitchen. You believe he's old enough to clean up his own mess.

> *Sometimes the reason children misbehave is simply because they don't know what you expect of them... Often, a polite request is enough to influence a child to change behavior.*

The first step is to politely make your desires known through a request. In this case, your polite request might be:

"Daryl, from now on, please do me a favor and bring your dishes to the sink when you're through with your snack."

If he agrees, be sure to add:

"Thanks, that'll be a big help. I appreciate your consideration of my time."

At times parents may become so frustrated with a misbehaving child that they forget to be respectful. A stepparent in the situation described above could easily wait until she's fed up with being treated like a servant, harbor her resentment inside for another week to let it really fester, then burst out with, "I'm sick and tired of having to pick up your mess! Do you think I'm your personal servant? If you weren't so lazy and inconsiderate…" This kind of outburst isn't likely to produce responsibility, cooperation, or dishes in the sink. Worse, your fit of temper could erase hard-earned progress toward building a bond with your stepchild.

If your child complies with your polite request but slips up later, you can offer a friendly reminder:

> *"Daryl, I noticed you forgot to put your dirty dishes in the sink. Please come get them."*

When a child repeatedly forgets or ignores an agreement, then a stronger communication tool is called for.

"I" Messages

"I" messages, a term coined by the late psychologist Thomas Gordon, are firm and calm communications that can produce surprisingly effective results. They are called "I" messages because they shift the emphasis from blaming the child (a traditional "you" message) to how the parent ("I") feels about the child's behavior. The benefits of "I" messages are:

- *Allowing parents to say how they feel about the child's behavior without blaming or labeling the child*

- *Creating a situation in which your child is more likely to hear what you're saying because you express it in a non-threatening way*

- *Conveying clearly to your child an important consequence of her behavior: your feelings*

- *Putting the emphasis on your child's behavior rather than on the child's personality*

- *Describing clearly to the child what behavior you want*

Since "I" messages work best in a firm and calm tone of voice, avoid using them when you're too angry.

When to Use an "I" Message

"I" messages are only effective when the adult owns the problem. When a polite request has failed to change behavior, an "I" message is a more assertive next step.

Since "I" messages work best in a firm and calm tone of voice, avoid using them when you're too angry. Allow yourself a cooling-off period, and then approach your child when you've regained control. An angry "I" message can easily trigger rebellion in a power-seeking child.

How to Send an "I" Message

There are four parts to an "I" message.

1. **Name the behavior or situation you want changed.** In order to avoid attacking your child's self-esteem, it's important to "separate the deed from the doer." It isn't that the child is bad, only that you have a problem with something the child is doing. By beginning with a statement aimed at the behavior, you avoid attacking the child's personality and self-esteem. You begin with "I have a problem with..." For example:

   "I have a problem with your leaving dirty dishes in the den."

2. **Say how you feel about the situation**...and say it without raising your voice. This lets the child know that the problem is serious to you. Although parents often use the word "angry" to describe their feelings, this often masks other emotions, mainly "fear" and "hurt." Children can usually hear us better when we're expressing emotions that are not threatening to them. "I feel concerned" or "I feel hurt" may be both closer to the truth and more effective than a statement of anger. This part of the "I" message begins with "I feel..." For example:

   "I feel taken advantage of..."

3. **State your reason.** Nobody likes to be treated as if he were expected to be blindly obedient. If you're going to change what's comfortable to you to please an authority, you at least want that authority to have a good reason for asking you to make the change. Children feel this just as strongly as adults do. A simple explanation about how your child's behavior is interfering with your needs, or the needs of the situation, can go a long way. For example:

> *"...because I have to spend time and energy cleaning up behind you."*

4. **Say what you want done.** You've already made a polite request or two, so now you're getting more assertive. This means letting the child know exactly what you'd like done. Remember, you get more of what you ask for than what you don't ask for. This step can begin with "I want" or "I would like." For example:

> *"When you leave the den, I want you to bring your dirty dishes to the kitchen and put them in the dishwasher."*

Putting this "I" message all together, we have:

> *"I have a problem with your leaving dirty dishes in the den. I feel taken advantage of because I have to spend time and energy cleaning up behind you. When you leave the den, I want you to bring your dirty dishes to the kitchen and put them in the dishwasher."*

Making "I" Messages Stronger: Two Variations

1. **Getting agreement.** You can make an "I" message even stronger by getting an agreement from your child about the behavior you want changed. This can be done by simply adding the question, "Will you do that?" and then not moving until you get a "yes." Eye contact strengthens it more. Saying "yes" also verbally commits the child to action and helps motivate her to follow through later. This can also be done by changing the last step of the "I" message from "I would like ..." to "Will you please ..." For example:

"I have a problem with your leaving dirty dishes in the den. I feel taken advantage of because I have to spend time and energy cleaning up behind you. Please bring your dirty dishes to the kitchen and put them in the dishwasher when you're finished. Will you do that?"

2. **Establishing a time frame.** Every parent knows the frustration of getting an agreement from a child about doing something, finding it still undone hours later, and confronting the child only to hear the refrain, "I'll do it." The implication, of course, is "I'll do it when I get around to it," and that may not occur in this decade. Your solution is to get a clear agreement as to when the behavior will be completed. In the above example, the "when" is built into the phrase "when you're finished." Other times, it can be added right after the child agrees to the request by simply asking, "When?" or by specifying a time.

Firm Reminders

When a child doesn't respond to a polite request or an "I" Message, your next step is to give a short but firm reminder. By suspending the rules of grammar and syntax, you give the message additional "oomph." For example:

"Dishes. Sink. Now!"

The fewer words you use, the better. This means avoiding the temptation to give a lecture on responsibility.

The fewer words you use, the better. This means avoiding the temptation to give a lecture on responsibility. Just make solid eye contact and firmly remind your child about what you want done—and when.

Your child may very well spring into action, amazing you and surprising himself in the process. If so, build on this success, as always, by encouraging him with a "thank you." However, some kids seem to need a lot of reminders, in which case it may be time to move on to the more advanced discipline methods: the rack and the screw. (Just kidding! In this edition, these medieval methods have been replaced with logical consequences and the FLAC Method.)

Logical Consequences

In order to influence your child to change from a negative behavior to a positive one, first she needs clear information from you about what change is expected. The basic discipline methods just covered provide the clear, firm communication to do this. However, sometimes children need to experience a more concrete consequence of their actions in order to learn the lesson of responsibility. Remember:

Responsibility = Choice + Consequence

You've already seen how reward and punishment as consequences can often backfire. The use of logical consequences offers an advanced form of discipline that is more consistent with life in today's society. A logical consequence can be defined like this:

LOGICAL CONSEQUENCE:
Discipline that logically connects to a misbehavior and is applied by an authority to influence a child to behave within the limits of the situation

Consequences are powerful teachers about the effectiveness of our choices and behavior. Better than a punishment or lecture, consequences offer parents their prime discipline tools. There are two types of consequences: natural consequences and logical consequences. For now, let's concentrate on logical consequences.

Examples:

> *When Daryl continues to forget to bring his dirty dishes into the kitchen after snacking in the den, he loses the privilege of taking food out of the kitchen.*

When Carly refuses to put away her toys, her stepmother puts them in the closet, out of reach, until the next day.

When Dennis The Menace® uses crayon on the wall, he must use his time and energy to wash it off.

Logical Consequences Vs. Punishment

Logical consequences aren't the same thing as punishment, even though your child will usually experience both as unpleasant. Some of the differences include:

Logical Consequences	Punishment
Are logically connected to the misbehavior	Is an arbitrary retaliation for the misbehavior
Are intended to teach responsible behavior	Is intended to teach blindly obedient behavior
Are administered in a firm and calm manner	Is often delivered in an atmosphere of anger and resentment
Respect the needs of adults and kids equally	Disrespects the child by implying that the adult's needs are more important
Allow the child to participate	Is dictated by the authority

Either/Or and When/Then Choices

Learning how to handle responsibility involves learning how to make good decisions. Logical consequences should therefore always be presented in the form of a choice. The consequences of children's choices teach them how to make better choices in the future. Parents can help children in this learning process by showing them that misbehavior is one of their choices, but that it carries a price: negative consequences. You also need to emphasize to your

Born Again

children that positive choices yield positive consequences. There are two types of choices you'll find extremely useful:

Either-or choices:

> *"Either you may _____ or you may_____ . You decide."*

When-then choices:

> *"When you have _____ , then you may _____ ."*

Either/or choices are particularly effective when you want your child to *stop* a misbehavior:

> *(Katherine leaves her belongings scattered around the kitchen in the afternoon.)*
> *"Katherine, either put your things away when you come home from school, or I'll toss them in a box in the basement. You decide."*

Notice that the logical consequence of leaving her belongings lying around is the inconvenience of having to dig them out of a junk box in the basement.

> *(Calvin continues to forget to put his dirty clothes in the hamper.)*
> *"Calvin, either put your dirty clothes in the hamper, or wash them yourself.."*

The logical consequence of not putting his dirty clothes in the hamper is that he must do his own laundry.

When/then choices are effective when you want to motivate your child to *start* a behavior:

> *(Maria has trouble getting her homework done and likes to spend time chatting online with her friends.)* *"Maria, when you've finished your homework, then you may go online."*

Notice that the logical consequence of not doing her homework is losing the privilege of using the computer. However, by phrasing the consequence positively, as a when/then choice, the options are more attractive to the child, and she is more likely to be motivated to finish the homework.

(Tom wants to go play in the backyard, ignoring his regular Saturday chore of cleaning his room.) "Tom, when you've cleaned your room, then you may go play outside."

It's easy to accidentally turn a logical consequence into a punishment. The following examples are poorly expressed because they're couched in negative terms: "Don't do that or else…" They can easily be seen as punishment—especially when accompanied by a harsh tone of voice and aggressive body language.

Poor examples:

> "Katherine, put your things away or I'm going to throw them in a box in the basement!"

> "Calvin, if you don't start putting your dirty clothes in the hamper, you're washing them yourself."

> "Tom, you may not go play outside until you have cleaned your room."

Guidelines for Using Logical Consequences

The following guidelines will help ensure that you're really using logical consequences and not punishment. They may seem like a lot to remember, but as you practice using them, these guidelines will become second nature.

1. **Ask the child to help set the consequences.** Since life in our democratic society encourages the participation of all those concerned with a problem, you'll stand a much better chance that your child will cooperate with your authority if you include her in the decision-making process. You'll be surprised how often the child will come up with choices and solutions that you wouldn't have thought of alone. For example:

"Katherine, I still have a problem with you leaving your belongings all over the kitchen. What do you think we can do to solve it?"

Even if the child has no helpful suggestions or is uncooperative about finding a solution, the important thing is that you asked. Since you have invited the child's participation, she'll be less likely to think of you as a dictator and to rebel against your authority. Of course, you'll want to come to the discussion prepared with your own logical consequences in case your child has no ideas.

2. **Give the child a choice.** If your child has a choice in the matter, she's much more likely to choose the positive behavior than if you gave her no choice. Use either/or and when/then choices. Remember, either/or choices work well when you want to stop a misbehavior, and when/then choices are useful when you want to encourage a positive behavior.

3. **Make sure the consequences are really logical.** One key to the success of logical consequences is that it's logically connected to the misbehavior. Children are better able to see the justice of such consequences and will usually accept them without resentment. However, if the consequence you select isn't really related to the child's behavior, it will come across as a punishment.

Not Logical:

"Either come in to dinner when I call or no TV for a week."

"Either play quietly while I work or I'm not taking you to the movie we planned."

"Either stop fighting or you'll both get a spanking."

Logical:

"Either come in to dinner when I call or it'll get cold——and you may miss it altogether!"

"When it gets quiet enough for me to finish my work, then I'll continue so that we'll be able to make it to the movie on time."

"Either stop fighting or the two of you will have to play in separate rooms."

Be sure that it's clear to children how a consequence is logically connected to their misbehavior. For example, you might make a family agreement that if someone doesn't complete a chore by the set time, then someone else may do that chore for him, and he must pay that person out of his allowance. But first you need to be sure that the children understand that allowance is connected to chores in a logical way: kids must earn their allowance by completing the week's chores.

4. **Only give choices you can live with.** There are many potential logical consequences for any given problem. Brainstorming with other parents, your spouse, or even the child is a great way to generate ideas about consequences, but when you own the problem, it's up to you to decide which choices to give your child. Only give choices you can accept. For example, if your child continues to forget to put his dishes in the dishwasher, a choice might be:

> *"Either put your dishes in the dishwasher, or I'll leave them in the sink and there will be no clean dishes."*

Your own values and desires are important. It's much better to keep thinking until you can come up with a consequence that won't punish you.

However, if you know a sink full of dirty dishes will drive you crazy, then don't give him this choice. Why? Because you'll likely sabotage the consequences by getting angry as the dishes pile up or end up putting them in the dishwasher yourself. In addition, your own values and desires are important. It's much better to keep thinking until you can come up with a consequence that won't punish you. For example:

> *"Either put your dirty dishes in the dishwasher or hire me as your servant to do it for you. How much do you pay?"*

> *"Either put your dishes in the dishwasher or I'll serve the next meal without dishes."*

By the way, parents who have used that last consequence say it takes only one meal of spaghetti eaten off a bare table by hand to teach the lesson. However, once again, if you couldn't live with the mess (or if you suspect that your children might prefer to eat with their hands!), then don't offer this particular choice. A consequence that works for one family may not be acceptable for another.

5. **Keep your tone firm and calm.** When giving the choice, as well as later when you enforce the consequence, it's essential that you remain both firm and calm. An angry tone of voice (the dictator's pitfall) invites rebellion and a fight. On the other hand, a wishy-washy tone of voice (the doormat's pitfall) suggests to the child that you don't really mean what you say. This invites noncompliance. In a democratic society, a firm and calm tone used by an authority figure says, "I recognize that you have a right to be treated respectfully, but you're out-of-bounds here. My job is to help you learn to stay in bounds, and I plan to do my job."

Your child must see that the choice results in a consequence. This lesson must be clear, or the value becomes diminished..

6. **Give the choice one time, then act to enforce the consequence.** For a logical consequence to teach a lesson, it must be enforced. If your child continues to choose to misbehave, then immediately follow through with the consequences. One way or another, children always choose. Even if they don't respond verbally, their behavior will tell you what they have chosen. Don't give the when/then or either/or choice a second time without putting the consequences into effect immediately. Your child must see that the choice results in a consequence. This lesson must be clear, or the value becomes diminished. For example:

   "If your books were in the kitchen when I cleaned, then you'll find them in the junk box in the basement."

7. **Expect testing.** When you attempt to redirect a child's misbehavior from negative choices towards positive ones, expect her to continue to misbehave for a while. The child is testing to see if you'll really do what you say you'll do. In other words, will you change your behavior? When a child rebels against her new stepdad, she's testing him—testing his staying power, testing how much he'll let her get away with, or perhaps testing the limits of his temper. That stepfather may not realize it, but by losing his temper, he's actually giving his stepdaughter the payoff she wants. And whether you realize it or not, when your children and stepchildren test you, they get some pay-off from your old way of responding, and they'll likely try to get you to revert to what you usually do. Even a punishment

can have a hidden pay off. As an active stepparent, you should expect that your child or stepchild may continue to misbehave for a while as a test of your commitment to the family. If you consistently enforce the consequences, soon he'll see that his testing isn't working, and he'll change his behavior. After all, children don't continue doing what doesn't work.

8. **Allow the child to try again after experiencing the consequences.** Since the goal is for your child or stepchild to learn from the consequences of his choice, opportunities must be provided to try again—but only after he's experienced the logical consequence. For example, Tom has agreed that when he's cleaned his room on Saturdays, then he may go play outside. His stepfather sees Tom heading out the back door before the room is cleaned and reminds him of his obligation.

If the child repeats the misbehavior after experiencing the consequences, then he may be testing. One can meet this challenge by stepping up the consequences after the second try, and stepping them up more after the third. For example, if Tom starts heading outside again next week without doing his chores, Stepdad can say:

"I see you've decided not to play outside this morning. Take care of your room and we can try again this afternoon."

Read the following story about a young stepmother's attempt to set a logical consequence for her stepdaughter's misbehavior. As you read, think about how the eight guidelines for logical consequences could have improved the experience for both the stepmom and the stepdaughter in this story.[1]

---

2 Stepmom is actually Elizabeth Einstein. This is a true story from her early days as a stepmother.

My two stepdaughters, Beverly and Brenda, had very different housekeeping standards: Brenda was a neatnik, and Beverly couldn't have cared less about tidiness. And yet, when we made our stepfamily, the girls had to share a room. This arrangement created problems from the start. The sisters had regular battles over Beverly's refusal to clean her side of the room. Often Brenda would beg me to "make" Beverly clean up the mess. Not understanding that the problem was theirs to settle, I'd intervene. I didn't know then what I know now: that siblings learn to negotiate and compromise by working together to solve problems such as this.

Finally, after many unsuccessful attempts to solve the problem for them, I lost it and shouted at Beverly, "Either you keep this room tidy or you can move your bed and belongings to the basement! Think about it and make your choice. I've had enough of this arguing!" I'd read about the importance of offering kids choices, so I thought this was the solution to the problem. When Beverly chose the basement, I figured it wouldn't take many nights in that lonely place for her to learn her lesson about tidiness and move back upstairs with Brenda.

But what I didn't count on was how Beverly would turn her choice to move to the basement against me. Her motivation was power and revenge. With her biological mother missing from her life, she often projected her anger onto me. In this case, she started telling her friends that I made her live in the basement. Of course, she didn't mention that she wasn't sleeping on rags in a corner; rather, she had a dresser, her bed, a carpet, and even posters on the wall. And, of course, she probably didn't tell her friends how this had come to be.

After a couple of weeks, I asked Beverly if she wanted to move back upstairs. Did she think she could be more respectful of her sister's shared space? Nope! She said she liked it down there.

Shortly after that, the school called to check out the "wicked stepmother" story that was circulating about me. Talk about embarrassing! Even as I explained how Beverly had chosen the basement over keeping her room clean, I wished I'd developed a different consequence. But I learned my own lessons from the experience: you have to be prepared to deal with how your consequence is viewed.

Logical Consequences Guidelines

1. Ask the child to help choose the consequence.

2. Give the child a choice: Either/Or choice or When/Then choice

3. Make sure the consequence is logical.

4. Give choices you can live with.

5. Keep your tone firm and calm.

6. Give the choice one time, then act.

7. Expect testing.

8. Allow the child to try again later.

Stepfamily Enrichment Activity: Teaching a Skill

Part of developing self-esteem and courage is seeing oneself as a capable individual. When you take the time to teach your child or stepchild a skill, you help her become more capable and powerful. In fact, teaching your child a skill can affect both of you in a very positive way by raising the child's self-esteem and enriching your relationship with her.

The following steps can help you teach a skill effectively:

1. **Motivate.** Encourage your child to want to learn the skill by explaining the value it has to the child or the entire family. For example:

   "Once you learn how to make your own sandwich for lunch, you won't always have to wait for me. Maybe sometimes you could even help me make lunch for everyone."

2. **Select a good time.** Pick a time when neither you nor your child will be rushed or upset by other things.

3. **Break the skill into baby steps.** When skills are learned one step at a time, there are more successes to help build courage and motivation.

For example:

"The first step is to get all of the ingredients out on the counter: the bread, the peanut butter, the honey, and a knife."

4. **Demonstrate.** Show your child how to perform the skill, explaining slowly as you do. For example:

"Next, watch how I dip the knife into the peanut butter, then slowly spread it onto a piece of bread."

5. **Let your child try.** Let your child perform the skill while you stand by, ready to offer help if he needs it. Be gentle about mistakes, and let it be fun. For example:

"Okay, now you try it. Just dip the knife in the jar so that you get plenty of that yummy peanut butter on it."

6. **Encourage…encourage…encourage!** Make plenty of encouraging comments that acknowledge your child's efforts and results. This builds self-esteem and keeps his motivation high to continue learning. For example:

"Great! That's the way to do it."

7. **Enjoy using the skill together.** Once your child has learned the skill, you can use it together and get companionship and satisfaction from the process. For example:

"This looks like the best sandwich ever. Let's eat!"

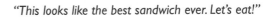

Marriage Enrichment Activity: Supporting your Partner

Parenting takes teamwork in any family, but it's essential in a stepfamily. It's especially important that partners support each other as they try to master the challenges of stepfamily discipline and that they learn to consider the stepfamily as a whole instead of prioritizing their biological relationships. Criticism and discouragement from a partner only make a stepparent's job harder, and siding with a child or disagreeing about discipline in front of a child not only demonstrates weakness in the marital bond but also sets the stage for future misbehavior. As a biological parent in a stepfamily, try to be there for your stepparent partner. Listen well, and offer encouragement and support.

The chart on the next page shows two kinds of responses that a biological parent can give in a conflict situation with his partner and his biological child. Try putting yourself in the stepparent's shoes and see which one you'd prefer.

Make it your goal to reduce and eventually eliminate reactive responses and instead become an active partner who uses active communication skills.

Take a close look at the way you and your partner work together as a team. First determine if you have "reactive" tendencies. Using the chart on the next page as a guideline, evaluate the way you respond when your partner makes a request, proposes an idea, or asks you a question. Make it your goal to reduce and eventually eliminate reactive responses, and instead become an active partner who uses active communication skills. As you start improving your communication with your partner, and as you begin supporting each other's discipline efforts, you'll begin seeing more cooperation from your children and find yourself in a more satisfying couple relationship.

Supporting Your Partner, the Stepparent to Your Children

Stepparent Says	Reactive Partner Responds	Active Partner Responds
Your daughter just screamed at me, "You're not my mother. I don't have to do what you say." I've had it. Do something or I'm out of here.	Don't freak out! She didn't mean it.	I know it hurts to hear her say that, but try not to take it personally. She's been through a lot and I guess she feels like taking it out on someone. I'll talk to her and try to find out what's going on in her head.
Your kid forgets his gym gear again and you drive across town to deliver it to him like you're his servant. How is that teaching him responsibility?	What am I supposed to do, let him flunk gym? Why are you acting so crazy? You just don't like me going near my ex-husband. Is that it?	You're right. I pamper him because I still feel so guilty about the divorce. But I shouldn't let my guilty feelings get in the way of teaching him responsibility. Next time I won't give in. Thanks for reminding me.
Your daughter borrowed my daughter's best jeans again without asking. Now they're fighting again. It never stops. I can't stand this bickering much longer.	Your daughter does the same thing. Besides, we all live in the same house. We should learn to share. What's the big deal?	It looks like we need to come up with an official set of rules about space and possessions in this household. Let's try to set rules that everyone can live with.
I nurture, I encourage, and still your kids don't like me. And truthfully, I don't love them like you need me to, either. This just isn't working. I hate letting you down like this.	Love me, love my kids. I told you that when we married. It's not asking that much. Are you backing out of the deal now? Can't you try harder?	Stop worrying about loving them. It was unrealistic for me to ask that of you. I hope you'll forgive me. Just keep accepting and respecting them, like you've been doing.

Chart adapted with permission from *Strengthening Your Stepfamily* (Einstein and Albert, Impact Publishers, 2006).

Family Meeting: Problem-Prevention Talk

Prevention is powerful! Many conflicts and misunderstandings can be avoided if you'll take the time to discuss guidelines and expectations before the situation occurs. Children often misbehave simply because they don't know what you expect from them. We've discussed this earlier when we presented information on boundaries and expectations that need to be clarified early in the development of your stepfamily. In other words, the children in your new stepfamily may not know where the limits are and how much freedom they're allowed in their new family. These expectations may differ vastly from what they knew in their previous family. When you work these issues out together in the early stages of your stepfamily life, you'll prevent lots of problems. Of course, many a shrewd child will intentionally stay in the dark about the rules, operating on the belief that "it's easier to gain forgiveness than permission." In any case, many conflicts and misunderstandings can be prevented if you'll take the time to discuss guidelines and expectations before a situation occurs.

Problem prevention isn't about laying down the law. You'll find that you can be much more effective as a parent or stepparent if you'll discuss potential problems with the whole family and decide how they can be prevented. As parents, you'll have certain limits that are non-negotiable. For example, it's not an option to leave your five-year-old stepson in the car rather than risk him misbehaving at the grocery store. But a willingness to be flexible within those limits can go a long way towards winning cooperation and avoiding problems. For example, before you take your five-year-old stepson grocery shopping with you, have a discussion with him about problems that might occur. He might get bored or uncomfortable. He might want you to buy everything within his reach. Discussing these issues before you leave home can improve your chances for having a problem-free outing and may save you a lot of time—and stress—in the store.

Use the following steps to make your problem-prevention discussion as effective as possible:

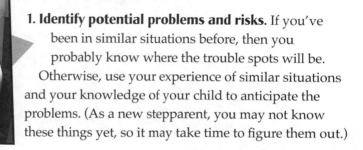

1. Identify potential problems and risks. If you've been in similar situations before, then you probably know where the trouble spots will be. Otherwise, use your experience of similar situations and your knowledge of your child to anticipate the problems. (As a new stepparent, you may not know these things yet, so it may take time to figure them out.)

For example, your stepchild whines for you to buy him a toy whenever you're in a store together. He also has a tendency to wander off, forcing you to chase after him.

2. **Share thoughts and feelings**. Ask your child what he thinks about the situation. Is he happy about it? Can he think of any problems that might come up? This will give you useful insight into why the child might misbehave. It will also help develop the bond between the two of you. After you hear his side, be sure to respond with empathy and make clear your own thoughts and feelings in a non-threatening manner.

   For example, your child may feel that shopping is boring and he'd rather be outside playing. You might say:

   "I know that shopping isn't much fun. I'd rather be outside in the garden or reading a good book, myself! But buying food for our family is my responsibility just like the chores you have. I have to do it so that we all have food to eat this week."

3. **Generate guidelines for behavior (making the situation a win-win for both of you).** Using the information you gathered in step two, talk with your child about what you expect. When discussing guidelines, keep in mind that it's easier to comply with the rules if you can make the situation enjoyable. We aren't suggesting the use of rewards or bribes for cooperative behavior, but well-thought-out incentives often work wonders with kids.

   For example, avoid:

   "If you'll be good, I'll buy you a toy."

   This is a bribe or a reward, and will lead to you having to buy the child something every time you go to the store.

   Better:

   "If we get our shopping done on time, we'll have time to stop by the park on the way home."

Best:

> *"How would you like to help me do the shopping by handing me the groceries off the shelf? Maybe you can help me decide some things you'd like to have for dinner."*

> *"Great! I also need for you to stay beside me all the time so that you'll be safe and we won't interfere with other shoppers."*

Many children will be more likely to follow the guidelines if they know what will happen if they violate them.

4. **Decide on logical consequences for violating the guidelines (if necessary).** Many children will be more likely to follow the guidelines if they know what will happen if they violate them. You don't need to use this step with children who are basically cooperative or who haven't had problems in similar situations. In fact, such a warning may seem like an insult to a child who only needs to be included in the discussion and have his needs considered in order to cooperate. For more challenging kids, however, consequences are very helpful when done correctly.

For example:

> *"When we get to the store, either stay close to me or else I'll have to put you in the cart."*

5. **Follow up later.** In situations in which you're not around to ensure that the guidelines were followed, you'll need to check up to see how your child behaved. If she has followed the guidelines, you can encourage her by acknowledging the good effort. Here's a great chance for a biological parent to compliment his daughter when his new wife reports that the child behaved well during an outing. That lets the stepchild know that, indirectly, the praise came from her stepmother—an incentive for her to repeat the good behavior next time. If she hasn't behaved well, then you'll need to enforce the logical consequences.

For example:

> *"Tamika, we agreed that you'd put away your toys before dinner or I'd take them away for two days. I just want to let you know that you can have your toys back on Monday."*

Summing It Up

■ Discipline that uses reward and punishment is outdated and ineffective.

■ Effective discipline requires specific tools: polite requests, "I" messages, and firm reminders.

■ Child discipline in a typical stepfamily is similar to discipline in a traditional, intact family in some ways, and significantly different in many other ways. Active parents want to help each other learn and heed these differences.

■ The authority to discipline stepchildren needs to be formally transferred to stepparents by the biological parent in the family.

■ Logical consequences for misbehavior teach kids cooperation and responsibility more effectively than threats, criticism, and punishment.

■ Either/or and when/then choices are effective methods of putting logical consequences into action.

■ When children live between two households, it's unrealistic to expect consequences given in one household to be carried over to the other household.

■ A problem-prevention talk is an effective way for a stepfamily to address an area of conflict.

■ Teaching a skill to a child or stepchild is a great way to strengthen the relationship and the child's self-esteem.

Chapter 4

HOME ACTIVITIES

- Practice using polite requests, "I" messages, and firm directions. Complete the guide sheet on page 154.

- Practice using logical consequences instead of punishment. Do the guide sheet on page 155.

- If you feel ready, conduct a "transfer of authority to discipline" from a biological parent to a stepparent.

- Have a problem-prevention talk to address a potential problem in your stepfamily. Report your results on page 157.

- Stepfamily Enrichment Activity: teach at least one of your children a skill this week.

- For your Marriage Enrichment Activity, practice supporting your partner in stepfamily conflicts.

Polite Requests, "I" Messages, and Firm Directions

1. Pretend that your child has just talked to you disrespectfully. Please write an example of a polite request that you could give your child:

_____

_____

2. Let's assume that your child continues to speak disrespectfully to you. Construct an "I" message that you could give your child:

I have a problem with _____

I feel _____

because _____

I would like (Will you please) _____

3. Let's assume that the "I" message was not effective. Construct a firm direction for your child:

_____

_____

Home Example

Write down a problem from your own family in which you own the problem. _____

_____

Now write an "I" message that you can use at home this week to solve the problem: _____

_____

When _____

I feel _____

because _____

I would like (Will you please) _____

Evaluation

How did your child respond to your "I" message? _____

_____

What did you like about the way you delivered the "I" message? _____

_____

How would you do it differently next time? _____

_____

Using Logical Consequences

Think of a problem you'd like to solve using a logical consequence. (You may choose the same problem for which you constructed an "I" message on the previous page as a back-up in case the "I" message is not effective.)

Write in the space below one way that you might present the choices and consequences to your child during the discussion of the problem. _____

_____

_____

Meet with your child to discuss the problem, and use this logical consequence or one that you develop with the child.

Evaluation

What was your child's response to the discussion? _____

_____

_____

What was his response to the logical consequence? (Did he test you to see if you would follow through?) _____

_____

If the consequence isn't working, do you think you need to stick with it longer or change the consequence to something else? _____

_____

If the consequence isn't working, have you violated any of the guidelines for setting up logical consequences? _____

What do you like about the way you handled the use of logical consequences? _____

_____

What will you do differently next time? _____

_____

Logical Consequences Video Practice

Scene	Guideline Violated	Possible Logical Consequences
1. Sherry *Matthew not getting up*		
2. Tim *Ben fighting*		
3. Grandma Sosa *Carlos and Javier fighting*		
4. Sherry *Angela not eating her peas*		

This worksheet refers to the Active Parenting for Stepfamilies *discussion program. If you are using this Parent's Guide independently and are interested in participating in a discussion group, check out the Parent tab at our website for a group being held near you.*
www.activeparenting.com

Family Meeting: Problem-Prevention Talk

Before having your talk...

What topic will you discuss?

_____

_____

What are some specific concerns or risks that you want to share your thoughts and feelings about?

_____

_____

_____

_____

After your talk...

What guidelines did your family decide upon?

_____

_____

_____

_____

_____

What logical consequences or incentives, if any, did you include?

_____

_____

_____

_____

What went well during the meeting?

_____

_____

_____

What will you do differently next time?

_____

_____

How will you follow up on the guidelines?

_____

_____

From Anger and Power Struggles to Courage and Self-Esteem

One day when our daughter Megan was a toddler, she stood up in her rocking chair. I looked at her and said, "Megan, rocking chairs are for sitting. Please sit down." And she looked at me with that look that says, "And what are you going to do about it if I don't?"

I f you're like most people, you would rather influence your environment than be influenced by it. You'd prefer to have some measure of control over every aspect of your life. You'd like for things to go your way, and you want the *power* to make that happen. As a parent or stepparent, you want to *empower* your children to develop their talents and skills and become competent individuals who contribute to the world. However, power is a double-edged sword. It can be used for better or for worse. Every parent knows the feeling of frustration that ensues when a child first learns to use her power to defy authority. So, when a child engages you in a power struggle, what ARE you going to do about it?

Here's what Megan's dad[1] did about it:

> *I decided that this might be a good place to use a logical consequence. So I said, "Megan, either sit in the rocking chair or I'll have to take it away for the rest of the day." She stood there and stared at me defiantly. I calmly picked her up, put her aside, and then took the chair out of the room. The next day when she stood in the rocking chair, I gave my daughter the choice, "You can either sit in the rocking chair or I'll have to take it away again." Megan sat down, having learned the lesson in one take.*

Just like adults, children want to have control over their environments. They, too, want the power to make things go their way. As they try to find that power in positive ways, sometimes children become discouraged and turn to rebellion, an easier way. Children can do this by trying to boss others

---

1   Megan's dad is Dr. Michael Popkin.

around or by showing others that they can't be bossed. After all, as every two-year-old knows:

The person in position to say "no" is in the more powerful position.

Rebellion and Power Struggles

That's why power struggles frustrate parents so much. You're bigger, smarter, more experienced, and in possession of the authority to decide what's in the best interest of your family, and still you cannot always make your children do what you want. They have the free will to choose, and if they choose to resist, your frustration can easily turn to anger. Feeling angry is the number one clue that you're in a power struggle and that your child has chosen a rebellious approach to attain her goal of power. The other clue is that power-driven children are very persistent and often respond to correction by continuing the misbehavior, often with open defiance. For example, consider a stepchild's threat, "No! You can't make me! You're not my father." How do you work with such a negative form of rebellion?

The first step is to recognize that your own behavior may be the "payoff" that keeps the child rebelling!

The first step is to recognize that your own behavior may be the "payoff" that keeps the child rebelling! Remember, many children of divorce have, in the past, been powerless over events that changed their lives, and they might still be feeling a sense of powerlessness. Your child or stepchild may start a power struggle with you in an attempt to reclaim some power in her life. As you learned in Chapter 4, the testing of stepparents is a popular pastime for children in stepfamilies. A power struggle is another type of test—one that reveals to your stepchild how you act under pressure. Will you back off? Will you report her behavior to her mother and set up a "caught in the middle" scenario, or will you work it out together? Be aware that the child may be trying to provoke a particular response from you such as losing your temper. That response is the child's "payoff."

You may be tempted to fight fire with fire. If you tend towards the autocratic style of parenting, threats such as, "No, you can't make me!" are fighting words. Hearing those words may hook your own desire for power by triggering thoughts such as, *I've got to be in control here…I'm the parent. I'm in charge!* And of course, *Oh yes I can!* But if you meet the child's challenge with a show of force, you'll wind up fighting, either verbally or with punishment. Ironically, the more you fight over power, the more your child or stepchild perceives that she's winning. After all, even if she eventually does what you want after a spanking, time-out, or other punishment, she still has the secondary payoff of knowing that she made you angry. This payoff reinforces your child's rebellious behavior. She might be thinking, consciously or not, *Look how powerful I am. I made him so mad!*

If you tend toward the doormat style, often you'll make the mistake of letting a rebellious child have his way. While your goal is just to avoid confrontation or to be liked, you'll end up giving in to the child's unreasonable demands and refusals, reinforcing his idea that rebellion works, and giving him the payoff that he was looking for. That payoff is that she gets her own way. Again, *look how powerful I am. I made my stepmother give in!*

Avoiding Power Struggles

The secret to avoiding a power struggle is to do the unexpected: neither fight nor give in.

This isn't an easy task, but with a little parent "judo," you can do it! The martial art of judo involves the skill of sidestepping your opponent's attack and then using your own thrust to throw him off balance. By doing the unexpected and not fighting—yet not giving in—you can influence your child to change some of the thinking that drives her behavior. First, you must stay calm and learn not to take rebellion personally (See the section on managing anger that follows). Of course it's hard not to personalize a child or stepchild's attack on you when it feels personal, but remember some of the dynamics at work here: children who have experienced loss such as divorce or the death of a parent may remain angry for a long time, and they might take it out on stepparents, siblings and step-siblings, and others who had no involvement in their past. Keep in mind that the child's very goal might be to anger you. Perhaps they want to make you feel as angry as they are! So the moment that you get angry, you lose the power struggle.

You can also "do the unexpected" by using the opportunity of a power struggle to communicate more confidence in your child's ability to make decisions by himself. Rather than boss, you can give choices.

> *"Would you rather put your dirty clothes in a hamper or in a laundry bag?"*

> *"Which PG movie would you like to watch?"*

You can let the child make some mistakes, and then experience the consequences—without lecturing or humiliating.

> *"Either put your dirty clothes in the hamper or you can choose to pay me a maid fee to pick up after you."*

> *"You can either watch a PG movie or there will be no movies at all. You decide."*

Consider this opportunity to "do the unexpected" a chance to change aspects of your parenting style with which you aren't happy.

You also can set up a stepfamily meeting to involve the child in making decisions that affect the whole family. Most importantly, you can show your child that you're not interested in fighting; rather, that you want to work together to find solutions. Let him know that you desire a cooperative relationship but, when discipline is necessary, you'll use logical consequences and other respectful methods, not anger and punishment.

Consider this opportunity to "do the unexpected" a chance to change aspects of your parenting style with which you aren't happy. If you're a doormat stepparent, realize that you *can* refuse to give in to the child's unreasonable demands. You *can* stop being a short-order cook, a wake-up caller, and a last-minute chauffeur. You *can* set firm limits, negotiate within those limits, refuse to be intimidated by displays of anger, and enforce the consequences of breaking the limits. All of these ideas require that you assert some of your own power and recognize your responsibility to be an active parent and leader in the family.

The FLAC Method

The acronym FLAC can help you remember how to defuse a power struggle without fighting or giving in. The letters stand for:

Feelings

Limits

Alternatives

Consequences

Let's use the following situation as an example. Nine-year-old Jason is angry about going to bed and keeps getting up for one thing after another. His father is about to get very angry when he remembers that getting angry and shouting at Jason is what his son expects because it's become a pattern. But he realizes that getting angry only fuels the power struggle between them. Instead, Jason's father does the unexpected. He sits down on his son's bed and says:

Father: I guess I really don't blame you for wanting to stay up later, Justin. I never liked going to bed, either. It feels like you're missing out on something, doesn't it? **(F for Feelings)**

Justin: (Surprised at his father's empathy) Yeah.

Father: Still, we all need our sleep to stay healthy and function well the next day, so you can't just stay up until you crash. **(L for Limits)**

Justin: But I don't want to go to bed now. It's too early.

Father: Hmm, well maybe there's an alternative. I'll consider letting you stay up an extra half hour if you use it as quiet time to relax yourself. Say, maybe by reading in bed. **(A for Alternative)**

Justin: Can I read fun stuff or does it have to be a schoolbook?

Father: You can read fun stuff. But here's the deal. If you get out of bed after the half hour is up, or if you're tired and cranky tomorrow or you don't get up on time, then tomorrow night it's back to your regular bedtime with no reading or hassle. Agreed? **(C for Consequences)**

Justin: OK.

Let's review the four steps:

Feelings: You've already learned how important it is to listen and respond to your children's feelings. When you show empathy for their feelings about the situation (and especially with your stepchildren, who may think you don't care about them), you suddenly move from being the enemy to being on their side in finding a solution to an acknowledged problem. This goes a long way towards defusing the power struggle while laying the groundwork for a win-win solution.

Limits: By reminding his son of the limits of the situation and providing a good reason for the limits, Justin's dad defined the problem to be solved ("don't give in"). Rather than saying, "because I said so," it's much less provocative to say, "because the situation calls for it." In this case, the situation calls for a good night's sleep.

Alternatives: Once you disengage from a struggle for power, you'll be surprised how often an acceptable alternative can be found. In Justin's case, the extra 30 minutes is unlikely to cause a problem (there's no magic number of minutes that every child needs to sleep), and it offers the additional benefit of encouraging the importance of reading. Like Justin's dad, you can make the limits more palatable for your child by negotiating within a reasonable range of options. Even when the limits are firm, often you can find an alternative within those limits that makes it more acceptable to the child.

Consequences: Some experts suggest that consequences only make matters worse with a rebellious child. Others recommend that parents come down even harder in a display of "tough love." However, if you can avoid getting angry (which turns a logical consequence into a punishment), then consequences can be useful as one more tool in motivating the child to live within the limits. They don't need to be harsh, just serious enough to remind your child that he's responsible for his actions and choices.

Parenting and Anger

In recent years, the subject of managing anger has gained status in our society. Now, everyone from your physician to the CEO of your workplace recognizes anger management as an essential skill for life in families, on the job, and throughout society. Anger that turns to rage and then to violence is responsible for the worst kind of news headlines: school shootings, terrorist attacks, family violence, and more. In your stepfamily, children and adults who cannot control their tempers create bad news in the form of pain and suffering for themselves and those around them. Yet anger is also a natural part of life, so we can't dismiss it altogether. The long and short of it is, nobody's quite sure what to make of this complicated emotion. Hopefully, these pages will give you a new view of an old subject.

The Anatomy of Anger

Response to frustration. Anger is an emotional and physiological response to frustration. If an important need or want is blocked for us, our bodies and emotions react with intense feelings that we often label as anger.

For example, a caveman walking through the woods comes upon a fallen tree that blocks his path. On the other side of the tree are some berries that he wants. He strains to push the fallen tree aside, but he isn't strong enough, and he becomes frustrated at the thought of not reaching his goal—to pick and eat those berries. His frustration produces physiological changes in his body that enable him to lift the fallen tree in a burst of energy and hurl it aside.

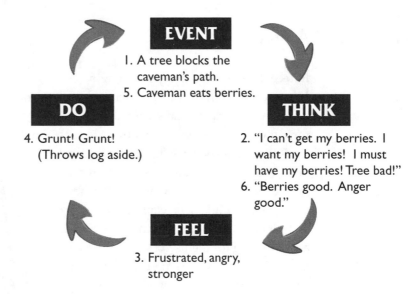

EVENT
1. A tree blocks the caveman's path.
5. Caveman eats berries.

THINK
2. "I can't get my berries. I want my berries! I must have my berries! Tree bad!"
6. "Berries good. Anger good."

FEEL
3. Frustrated, angry, stronger

DO
4. Grunt! Grunt! (Throws log aside.)

Purpose of anger. Anger releases certain chemicals into the bloodstream. These chemicals produce changes that make us stronger, faster, and more intimidating to others. This is known as the "fight or flight" response because this physiological reaction makes us ready to fight danger or run from it. In primitive times, when problems were settled by brute force, the added power that anger produced helped us to survive.

Old brain/new brain theory. Anger is associated with the so-called "old brain," which has been present in human beings since the beginning of our existence. But as the "new brain" has evolved around the old brain, so have human intelligence and societies based on law. This gives us the ability to handle problems with rational solutions rather than brute force.

"Use" not "lose" our temper. However, even in modern societies, anger sometimes pays off. Psychiatrist Rudolf Dreikurs, noted for his studies of the motivations behind children's misbehavior, once said that people do not "lose" their temper; they "use" their temper. What he meant was that people sometimes use anger to intimidate others into giving them what they want. Since anger is often accompanied by violence, this intimidation can sometimes be effective, but it carries a high price. Anger used to bully other people damages relationships and is hurtful. Worse yet, it can lead to violent behavior.

How to Use Anger Positively

The feelings that arise within you when you become angry tell you that one of your goals is being blocked. Anger clearly sends this message:

> *"Act! Don't just sit there; get up and do something!"*

If you do something soon, often you can solve the problem before it gets worse. If you don't act and, instead, try to ignore the message, several things could happen:

1. The problem might go away by other means, but this is a risky and uncertain possibility.

2. Your anger may grow in intensity until it propels you into some action, which is likely to be desperate, impulsive, and potentially violent.

3. Your anger may fester internally, expressing itself in unexpected ways: headaches, rashes, ulcers, depression.

There are several useful ways to listen to the message of anger and take positive action:

1. **Act to change the situation (Do something different).** Struggle until you remove the fallen tree. Example:

Use effective discipline skills such as "I" messages, logical consequences, and the FLAC method.

2. **Reduce the importance of the goal (Think something different).**
   Put it in perspective.

   Examples:

   Although you may want those delicious looking berries very much, be aware that you don't need them for your survival.

   Your stepchild refuses to take a bath. Remind yourself that your goal of a daily bath is less important than your developing relationship with her. Missing a bath won't seriously affect your stepchild's health.

3. **Change your goals (Again, think something different).** Find an alternative.

   Examples:

   Decide that the berries aren't the only solution to the hunger problem and look for an alternative—maybe an apple tree near the river.

   Give up your goal of having your stepdaughter play the piano and encourage an alternative activity that she chooses.

Helping Children Use Their Anger

Because children are usually more primitive than adults in their expression of emotions, often they'll resemble the caveman when experiencing frustration and anger. Tantrums and hitting are fairly common with young children. However, it's increasingly important in these days of "zero tolerance" for aggressive behavior that we teach children

that violence isn't an okay way to solve problems. There are several ways parents can help:

1. **Give them a good model.** The way you handle your own problems and frustrations provides a powerful model for your children and stepchildren.

   - *Do you fly into a rage, hurling insults and humiliating remarks?*

   - *Do you strike out at others?*

   - *Do you sink into a depression (an adult temper tantrum or "silent storm")?*

2. **Guide them with words to find more effective forms of expression.**

   Examples:

   "You have the right to feel the way you do, but in our family, we don't scream and blame. We look for solutions."

   "I see that you're angry. Can you tell me with words what you're angry about instead of hitting?"

   "When you get angry at me, please tell me without calling me names. I don't call you names."

When a child has a tantrum, you can acknowledge his anger, but at the same time, "take your sails out of their wind."

3. **Remove yourself from a power struggle.** When a child has a tantrum, you can acknowledge his anger, but at the same time, "take your sails out of their wind." Don't try to overpower the child; withdraw instead. This action says to the child, "I am not intimidated by your show of temper and will not give in, but I won't punish or humiliate you either." The result is that the child who gets neither a fight nor his own way after throwing a tantrum usually finds a more acceptable ways to influence people. For very young children, you can withdraw from the power struggle by simply not responding to the child and, instead, attending to your own business. For children who are old enough to be left alone in a room, do just that. If you need a quiet place to withdraw from the power struggle, try the bathroom—the one place where privacy is usually expected.

4. **Use the FLAC Method.** In those situations where a child's tantrum interferes with the rights of others (like in a restaurant, or when you have guests in your home), you can acknowledge the child's feeling, remind him of the limits, offer an alternative, and follow through with logical consequences.

For example:

> *"I know you're angry about having to go shopping with me, and I'll admit that it isn't much fun. Still, we do want to eat dinner tonight, so we need to get this done. How about if you help me out by putting the food in the cart? That'll make it go faster, and then you can help me pick out your favorite dessert."*

If the child continues to act out his anger, add a logical consequence:

> *"Dennis, you can either calm down and help me shop or we'll have to go sit in the car until you can. Then we definitely won't have time to stop by the park."*

Children must learn that there are consequences for violent and aggressive behavior. The child who acts out his anger by breaking something can help pay for its replacement. The child who hits or bullies can be removed from other kids for a period of time to think about how he can make it up to the other person—and not just with a mumbled, "I'm sorry," but with some sort of meaningful behavior. As with all logical consequences, stay calm and firm when delivering them. Your goal isn't to hurt the child, which may just begin a revenge cycle, but rather to teach him.

5. **Allow your child to influence your decisions.** When a person feels powerless to influence leaders, frustration gives way to anger and rebellion. If you don't allow your child to influence your decisions concerning her, she might use negative methods of influence such as tantrums, whining, or tears. The method your child uses to influence your decisions depends on what you allow to work. If you redirect your child to express his anger respectfully, listen to his arguments, and sometimes change your decisions, then your child learns the important skill of negotiation.

Courage … One from the Heart

While parents and children both need power to survive and thrive, they need a character filled with courage even more. In fact, preparing children to courageously meet the challenges that life offers is perhaps the single most important aspect of all good parenting. In today's complex world of choices, courage forms the very foundation upon which children construct their personality. Both psychologist Alfred Adler and world leader Winston Churchill said that courage is the most important of all traits because it's the one on which all others depend. From the French word *coeur*, meaning "heart," courage is the "heart" that enables you to take risks. And it's through risk-taking that you're able to develop responsibility, cooperation, independence, and whatever else you may strive for. We define **courage** in *Active Parenting for Stepfamilies* as:

COURAGE:
The confidence to take a known risk
for a known purpose

Courage is a feeling of confidence that motivates you to take risks, knowing that you have a chance to succeed and that, even if you fail, the risk was worth taking. Courage isn't the absence of fear but the willingness to take a reasonable risk in spite of fear. Without courage, you'd too often find yourself sitting on the sidelines, unwilling to take the risks inherent in any endeavor. You'd let life pass you by as you wishfully waited for someone else to do it for you.

Courage isn't the absence of fear but the willingness to take a reasonable risk in spite of fear.

When you're aware of the high divorce rate for remarried couples, your choice to create a stepfamily shows that you have courage to take a risk in spite of the challenges ahead. With your courage to make it work, combined with good parenting skills and a positive attitude, there's little reason you can't be successful in building a happy and peaceful stepfamily. In fact, research reveals that some of the negative effects of divorce can be reversed for children living in a healthy stepfamily. When you approach your role as a nurturing stepparent who encourages your children, you'll play a part in helping them heal their hearts and free their minds so that they can focus on the normal business of growing up.

Self-Esteem ... One from the Mind

Children aren't born with self-esteem; they develop it. Parents and stepparents can use skills of effective discipline, communication, and encouragement with children to help them develop this powerful attribute.

Where does courage come from? It comes from a belief in yourself that you're a lovable, capable human being who eventually will succeed. And even if you fail, you're still a lovable, capable human being able to recognize your strengths and weaknesses and be comfortable with that balance. This positive belief in yourself is commonly called "self-esteem." When you think well of yourself and believe that you have a good chance to succeed, then it makes sense that you'll have the courage to take risks. Children aren't born with self-esteem; they develop it. Parents and stepparents can use skills of effective discipline, communication, and encouragement with children to help them develop this powerful attribute.

High Self-Esteem → **COURAGE**

Courage usually produces positive behaviors, including the perseverance to keep trying when the going gets tough. Often the result is success and positive feedback from others, and that, in turn, helps to strengthen self-esteem and to build courage to create a success cycle.

SUCCESS CYCLE

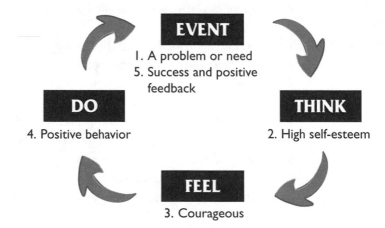

EVENT
1. A problem or need
5. Success and positive feedback

THINK
2. High self-esteem

FEEL
3. Courageous

DO
4. Positive behavior

As the graphic portrays, a success cycle doesn't mean that your children will never run into problems or failure; rather, they'll be able to handle these problems effectively and eventually succeed. The opposite of a success cycle might be called a failure cycle. When self-esteem is low, kids often lack the courage to take positive risks. They either don't try at all, or they take the easier route and use misbehavior to reach their goals. But misbehavior often leads to failure and produces negative feedback from others, which lowers self-esteem further and produces more discouragement in a downward spiral of failure.

FAILURE CYCLE

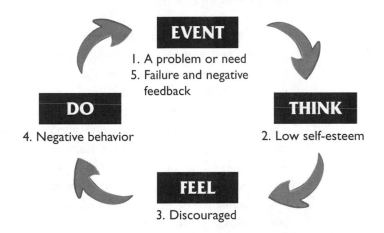

EVENT

1. A problem or need
5. Failure and negative feedback

DO

4. Negative behavior

THINK

2. Low self-esteem

FEEL

3. Discouraged

Children in stepfamilies may struggle with low self-esteem as they cope with all the losses and changes they've experienced during their family upheaval. Too often, adults are so engrossed in managing their own divorce process, or grieving the death of a partner, that they may be emotionally unavailable to guide their children through these tough times. Without realizing it, a parent can become part of a child's failure cycle. As an active parent or stepparent, however, you can have a great and positive influence on the children in your stepfamily.

The Power of Encouragement

What does the word *encourage* really mean?

Dividing the word into two parts, "en-courage" means to "instill courage." Rudolf Dreikurs once said, "children need encouragement like plants need water." Encouragement is the fertilizer that nourishes our children's courage, self-esteem, and character, and enriches their skill base. Wherever it's applied, more growth occurs in that area. Do you want your stepchild to be a good reader? Encourage her reading. Do you want him to be honest? Encourage acts of honesty. Where you sow encouragement, you spur growth and possibilities.

Where you sow encouragement, you spur growth and possibilities.

Fostering an encouraging environment in your home will help you and your stepfamily meet the challenges ahead. Think some more about "the beauty of problems," which we discussed in Chapter 2. Problems in your family open the door for encouragement. When your stepfamily faces a crisis, instead of letting the problem stop you on your path to success as a stepfamily, use it as an opportunity to make changes. Your choice to implement these changes rather than get bogged down in the problem will encourage your family (yourself included) to move ahead with a positive attitude. From this strengthened base, each future crisis or setback becomes easier to resolve because fear of failure is reduced. And as your own sense of encouragement grows and you begin to feel that your stepfamily is growing stronger, you'll recognize setbacks as merely setbacks rather than as a signs of failure.

The rest of this chapter helps you to strengthen your encouragement skills. These skills not only help to increase children's self-esteem and start a cycle of success, they also present many opportunities for new stepparents to build better bonds with their stepchildren and to strengthen every relationship in the family.

"Catch 'em Doing Good"

Imagine yourself as a new stepparent in this situation:

You're driving home from work. You've been worrying about how you're doing as a stepparent, especially in light of the argument you had with your stepdaughter last night. Then your husband phones and asks you to meet him at your favorite café to discuss an important matter. Anxiously, you change course and head towards the café, imagining the worst. By the time you reach the café, both your mind and your heart are racing. As you approach the restaurant door, your husband comes out to meet you. He tells you that he hired a sitter for the kids so the two of you can talk alone. Uh-oh, you think. Here it comes. He's upset about the argument. I've really blown it! I'm a terrible stepmother. Thoughts like these and the anticipation of what your husband will say make it hard for you to get through the process of being seated and placing your orders. But finally that business has been taken care of, and your husband begins.

"You know, I was worried about how my kids would take to you after losing their mother. That loss was so hard for them. It seemed unlikely that they'd let you into their lives. But I underestimated you. I want to congratulate you on your fine job of building a relationship with them in spite of how they dump their negative feelings onto you."

Is this for real? you ask yourself. Surely it must be a joke! But your husband seems perfectly sincere as he goes on to say, "If every new stepmother were as kind and patient as you, every child would want to be in a stepfamily. So I just wanted to thank you." He pulls out a small package tied with a ribbon and places it In your hand.

How do you think you'd react in this situation?

a. You'd feel great, and even a little proud of yourself.

b. You'd feel relieved that your assumption was wrong—that you aren't doing so badly as a stepmother after all.

c. You'd feel encouraged to doubt yourself less and not to fear the challenges of being a stepparent.

d. You'd almost faint from the shock!

While you'd probably experience all of the above reactions, chances are that response "d" is the closest to how you'd really feel. Once the shock wore off, you'd probably feel pretty good about yourself. You'd feel encouraged to continue being an active, nurturing stepparent, and you'd feel invigorated—ready for the next stepparenting challenge.

This is an example of the power of encouragement. With only a few words, your husband increased your self-esteem, boosted your confidence, and created the likelihood that you'd become an even better stepparent in the future. No wonder some call encouragement "the subtle giant."

You can probably think of many times during an average day when a word of encouragement from an important person in your life would mean a lot to you. Apply that thought from the perspective of a child, and realize that not only do children *like* to hear encouragement from their parents and step-parents, but they also *need* to hear it for all the reasons we've discussed so far in this chapter.

Encouraging children can be a simple matter. Elaborate planning and costly gifts aren't required. A few well-chosen words can work wonders.

Encouraging children can be a simple matter. Elaborate planning and costly gifts aren't required. A few well-chosen words can work wonders. Over the course of a day, you'll find many excellent encouragement opportunities. Just "catch 'em doing good" and let your children know that you appreciate them.

The downside of encouragement is that in every opportunity to encourage our children (as well as ourselves and others), there's also an opportunity to *dis*courage them or "remove courage." Because most of us aren't natural-born encouragers, we need to recognize our own discouraging tendencies as we try to strengthen our ability to encourage. Before we look further at encouragement, let's consider its opposite—discouragement—and the ways it affects children's behavior.

Avoid Discouraging

Children who misbehave are usually *discouraged*. Somewhere along the line, they've lost the courage to face life's problems with positive behavior. Traumas such as divorce and the death of a parent have tremendous power to discourage children, and all too often that's their state of mind at the start of their new stepfamily. While you can't erase the past, it will help for you to become aware of ways you or your partner might be discouraging your children. If you become a discouraging force in your child's life, you'll lower his self-esteem, which leads to discouragement, which prompts negative behavior.

Although abuse and neglect are the most serious forms of discouragement, we'll focus our attention on four less-obvious ways that parents sometimes discourage their children and how you can turn them into methods of encouragement.

Discouraging Events	Encouraging Events
Overprotection and pampering	Stimulating independence
Focusing on mistakes	Building on strengths
Expecting too little	Showing confidence
Expecting too much (perfectionism)	Valuing the child as-is

Overprotection vs. Stimulating Independence

Put yourself in your child's shoes for a moment. If somebody who's important to you spends too much time telling you how dangerous and difficult the world is, you may come to believe that you can't handle things for yourself. You may let him handle problems for you, depriving you of a chance to learn from the experience. If you get in trouble at school or with the law, he's there to bail you out. And if you never experience the consequences of your mistakes, you begin to get the idea that you can do anything you like. But strangely you don't feel very confident, although sometimes you may act overly confident to make up for your insecurity. Once you find that your parents will constantly wait on you and solve your problems, you begin to expect that treatment from others. When those others don't treat you the same, you find that things start falling through the cracks and mistakes multiply. You become angry and blame others, then wonder why your relationships aren't satisfying.

Statements such as these from parents and stepparents may be well intentioned, but they're counterproductive:

> *"Sure, I'll be glad to go to the school and talk to your teacher. I'm sure when she realizes how hard you worked, she'll change your grade."*

> *"I shouldn't have to call you three times to get up in the morning, but at least you're getting to school on time."*

How to Stimulate Independence

Independence is essential for thriving in our modern society. In fact, when you keep your children overly dependent on you, not only do they pay a price, but so do you. As psychologist Haim Ginott wrote, "Dependence breeds hostility." The last thing you want to do as parents and stepparents is to keep your children overly dependent on you. Your task as parents is eventually to work yourselves out of a job. The following important points will help you to stimulate your children's independence.

Avoid pampering. Pampering your children doesn't lead to the appreciation that many parents expect; it leads to resentment! A pampered child eventually becomes dependent, spoiled, or discouraged.

Some signs that you're pampering your child include: calling her more than once to get up in the morning; routinely driving her places on short notice; picking out her clothes; giving her money on demand instead of an allowance; allowing her to curse at you or otherwise speak disrespectfully; not monitoring media such as TV, music, movies, and the Internet; making her homework your responsibility; allowing her to frequently eat meals in front of the TV; always cleaning up after her; not requiring her to help with family chores; and rescuing her from the consequences of her misbehavior.

A better approach to preparing children for "real life" is to allow them to make mistakes, solve their own problems, and eventually forge a unique path to developing a courageous and responsible character.

Also be aware that certain stepfamily dynamics can contribute to a parent's tendency to pamper. If you're a parent of biological children in a stepfamily, you might be tempted to compensate for the hardship that the children have experienced—divorce, the death of a parent, or other tough transitions—by overprotecting and taking over their responsibilities. Perhaps you promised yourself, after the divorce, that you'd never again cause your children to go through such pain. It's a noble goal, but not a realistic one for two main reasons: first, by overprotecting, you're failing to prepare your children for the future. Second, in a stepfamily where you have stepchildren as well as biological children, catering to your own children will inevitably set the tone for resentment among siblings and mistrust of stepparents.

If you're a new stepparent, you might tend towards pampering your stepchildren for the simple reason that you want them to like you. Here you must put the children's welfare before your own. Also consider that any favor you win through pampering is not of the sincere and lasting sort; rather, your stepchildren might come to expect special treatment and misbehave unless they receive it.

In both cases, a better approach to preparing children for "real life" is to allow them to make mistakes, solve their own problems, and eventually forge a unique path to developing a courageous and responsible character.

If you've come to realize that you're pampering your children, then it's time for a change. Let your children know that you've decided to stop pampering them and that mutual respect is the new way of life in your stepfamily. You can do this in a firm yet friendly way, taking responsibility yourself while encouraging your children. For example:

> *"I want to apologize for treating you like you didn't have the good sense to handle _____ (e.g., getting yourself up in the morning; your own money; your own homework; picking up your own clothes). From now on I'm going to stop treating you like a baby and leave it up to you."*

> *"I don't use that kind of language when I'm angry with you; I don't expect you to use it when you're angry with me."*

> *"I'll be glad to show you where dirty clothes go, but from now on I'm only washing the clothes that get put in the laundry basket."*

Learning to work cooperatively with others is a key to individual success, stepfamily success, and community success.

Help children develop a sense of interdependence. Life in our diverse, modern society is neither independent nor dependent. It's interdependent. Learning to work cooperatively with others is a key to individual success, stepfamily success, and community success. Invite your children to engage in cooperative behavior with the aim of letting them experience the pleasure and benefits of group efforts.

> *"You're an important part of this stepfamily, and we'd like your ideas at stepfamily meetings."*

> *"Why don't you come sit with us instead of by yourself?"*

> *"Would you like to make lasagna with us?"*

Allow natural consequences to teach. Children learn an amazing number of valuable life lessons from direct experiences that happen naturally, without a parent's prompting or participation. This method of learning is called *natural consequences*.

Here are some examples:

> *The natural consequence of oversleeping on a school day is being late for school.*

> *The natural consequence of leaving your bicycle outside may be that it gets rusty or that it's stolen.*

Natural consequences are particularly effective for teaching independence because the parent or a stepparent can be a sympathetic third party rather than the disciplinarian. But avoid these temptations:

1. **Rescuing the child**

   For example, driving to your son's father's house with his baseball mitt because he forgot to pack it

2. **Saying, "I told you so."**

   It's so much more effective to say, "Gee, I know that's frustrating. Do you have some plan of how to replace your bike?" rather than "I told you this would happen if you didn't put it away!"

When Natural Consequences Cannot Be Used as Teachers

There are three circumstances in which a responsible parent cannot allow natural consequences to teach the lesson:

1. **When the natural consequences may be catastrophic.** For example, the natural consequences of running into a busy street may be death.

2. **When the natural consequences are so far in the future that the child isn't concerned about the connection.** For example, the natural consequences of not brushing her teeth may lead to eventual tooth decay.

3. **When the natural consequences of a child's behavior affect others rather than the child.** For example, your stepchild child borrows your scissors and loses them.

In these situations, the adults own the problem, and it's up to them to use the discipline skills covered in Chapter 4 to take action and prevent such natural consequences from occurring or reoccurring.

Building on Strengths vs. Focusing on Mistakes

Think about how you react to your children's efforts to improve themselves. Maybe your stepchild has worked hard to correct a problem or improve a behavior. Do you pick out the parts that still aren't right? Focusing on mistakes can have a devastating effect on a child: she may feel that you don't appreciate her effort, wonder why she should bother to try again, and fear she'll never meet your standards. Soon she may lose motivation, and her performance will drop further, prompting more discouraging comments from you until, finally, she feels like a certified loser.

> *"You left your glass in the den again last night! How many times do I have to ask you to be more considerate?"*

> *"This doesn't look good where you colored outside the lines, does it?"*

> *"Did you notice how your opponent beat you down court for that easy basket? You've really got to hustle back on defense."*

Building on Strengths

Kids need to know what mistakes they've made to learn from the experience and do better in the future. The error that parents make most often is to become masters at pointing out mistakes and misbehavior and ignoring successes and positive behavior. The key to building successful behavior, however, is to focus the majority of your feedback on what your kids do right. This positive attention builds their confidence and motivates them to keep improving.

Building on strengths is also an important factor as you develop relationships with your stepchildren. Stepparents who focus on a stepchild's mistakes won't go far in earning trust. Rather than picking out what your stepchild is doing wrong, look for things that she's done right, or simply things that you like about her. Even if you're having a hard time developing affection for your stepchild, there's bound to be something that you like about her: her quick wit, or bright smile.

Focusing your attention on what's right with your children, rather than what's wrong, is encouraging. As you've seen, encouragement leads to improved self-esteem, which leads to courage and positive behavior . . . in other words, a success cycle. So it's important to build on your children's and stepchildren's strengths as often as possible. The following four tips will help you incorporate this form of encouragement into your everyday life:

Take baby steps. A key to building on strengths is to break the learning down into baby steps. This makes the challenge less intimidating and provides more opportunities for encouragement. The first step should be to identify your goal.

> *"I know that homework can get overwhelming. Why don't we begin by making a list of your assignments and how long each will take?"*

Acknowledge what the child does well. Once you've identified a goal with the child, find out where he is on the path towards reaching that goal. Acknowledge what he can already do well in order to build his confidence and motivation to take the next step.

> *"Terrific! You've completed two assignments. I can see that you've really worked hard at this, but I already knew you could work hard . . . I've watched you on the basketball court."*

In addition to acknowledging progress towards the goal, this example illustrates how you can also use this positive response to recognize other areas where the child is already experiencing some success.

Nudge the child to take the next step. There are times for all of us when the frustration of not progressing the way we'd hope to undermines our courage to keep trying and tempts us to give up. This is when an encouraging nudge from a parent or stepparent can help give the child enough courage to take the next baby step. For example:

"Learning to do division can be frustrating, and I'd guess you feel like giving up. But if you'll just stick with it, I know you'll get it. Look how far you've come already! Now, how about tackling that last problem one more time?"

"Keep trying. You're getting it!"

"Sometimes a little time away from it can help. Let's try again tomorrow."

Keep encouraging improvement and effort. The mistake most people make in the encouragement process is to wait until the child attains a desired goal before offering encouragement. Any improvement, no matter how small, is a step in the right direction, and you should acknowledge that! Since success is a great motivator, you want your child to experience numerous smaller successes along the way. This builds self-esteem and keeps the child moving towards her goal. If your child or stepchild has a setback (and that's to be expected), she needs your encouragement to keep at it and not give up. In fact, even when she's not making progress, you should always encourage just her effort alone.

Any improvement, no matter how small, is a step in the right direction, and you should acknowledge that!

"Great! You're really getting good at keeping track of your assignments. One more day and you'll have done it for a whole week."

"I can really see the effort that you put into this."

"Hey, this room really looks good. You've picked up all your books and the bed's made. If you like, I could help you figure out a system for organizing your closet."

Showing Confidence vs. Expecting Too Little

Try to think like a child again. This time, consider how you'd feel if people who were important to you didn't believe in your ability to do anything well. You probably wouldn't believe in it either, would you? They don't have to say so; you can usually tell what they think of you by the way they act around you and the words they

use with you. If they never ask your opinion, you might guess that they don't think you have anything useful to say. If they seem satisfied with half-hearted efforts at school, you may figure they think that mediocrity is all you're capable of achieving. Of course, sometimes they make their opinions of you crystal clear by saying things like:

> *"No, you can't use that! You'll break it."*

> *"I guess you're just not the type who does well in school."*

> *"Maybe your mother never cared enough to teach you…"*

How to Show Confidence

When the people we value most show confidence in our abilities, we tend to gain confidence in ourselves.

A cornerstone of self-esteem and courage is the belief that we're capable of success, whether it's in school, at work, with friends and family, or in a love relationship. As we achieve success in solving life's problems and learning new skills, our belief in ourselves increases. But tackling problems and attempting new skills takes confidence. When the people we value most show confidence in our abilities, we tend to gain confidence in ourselves.

Parents and stepparents can help their children succeed by showing confidence in them. Here are some ways to do this:

Give responsibility. Giving a child responsibility is a way of showing confidence. It's a nonverbal way of saying, "I know you can do this." Of course, you'll want to give responsibilities that are in line with your child's age and abilities. Stepparents without children of their own must learn what's possible and normal for children of certain ages.

> *"I'll agree to your wanting to get a dog, Julie, if you'll accept the responsibility of feeding and caring for her."*

> *"I think you have handled getting yourself up in the morning really well, so you can probably manage staying up later now—say, 9:00 p.m. What do you think?"*

Ask your child's opinion or advice. Kids like to have parents and stepparents rely on their knowledge or judgment. When you ask your child's opinion, you demonstrate confidence in his ability to make a useful contribution. It also helps bolster his self-esteem and brings you closer together.

"Which route do you think would be best on our trip to visit Grandma?"

"Would you teach me how to play your new video game?"

"Well, what were the reasons for the Civil War?"

Avoid the temptation to take over. It's an act of confidence in your children's abilities when you refuse to step in and take over when they become discouraged. If you do something for your child on a regular basis that she, with a little persistence, could do independently, then you're communicating a lack of confidence in her abilities. Likewise, when you bail her out of the consequences of misbehavior, you'll rob her of an important lesson in responsibility. In effect, you're saying that you don't have confidence in her ability to handle the consequences of her actions.

All in all, taking over or helping too much actually certifies a child's discouragement and leads to an inability to tolerate frustration. When things don't work out immediately, they give up or throw a tantrum. Avoid this by encouraging your children to stick with it. Use words such as these:

"Keep trying. You can do it!"

"I can't stop the kids from teasing you, but let's talk about some things you can do."

Expect success and positive behavior. The expectations you have of your children hold a tremendous amount of power to influence their behavior. In fact, children often live up or down to parents' and stepparents' expectations. So, why not expect them to succeed? When you let them know that you think they can do it, you're encouraging them to live up to your expectations. Just keep in mind that sometimes they'll mess up, and then they'll need your encouragement not to give up. Here are some examples of how to make your expectations known to your children:

> *Children often live up or down to parents' and stepparents' expectations. So, why not expect them to succeed?*

"I know you can improve your grades if you set your mind on it."

"I'm counting on you to use your best manners when we're at Grandma's."

"I expect you to tell me the truth."

Valuing Children vs. Expecting Too Much (Perfectionism)

Positive expectations are important. So are realistic ones. If a parent expects more from a child than that child is able to give, the child may decide to make her mark in other ways. If she can't be the best at being the best, maybe she'll decide to be the best at being the worst. Or maybe, in a futile attempt to try to please her parent, the child will become a perfectionist. As she tries harder and harder to succeed, life becomes one big worry. But even when she does succeed, she can't enjoy her success for fear of what challenge her self-esteem faces next.

"How could you possibly misspell 'circus' when you got all the others right? If you'd really thought about it longer, you would have had a perfect paper."

"This isn't a bad report card. But with your potential, you could have done better."

How to Value Children

A child's self-esteem doesn't spring from achievements alone. What most of us—kids and adults included—really want deep down inside is to be accepted for just being ourselves, not for our achievements. This is what it means to feel a sense of belonging.

Think for a moment about the children in your stepfamily. They've been uprooted. They've experienced many changes: new siblings, new stepparents, loss of their old school and friendships. Chances are, they're feeling anxious and confused about where they fit in and if this new family accepts them for who they are.

Children who feel accepted by their parents have a solid foundation of self-esteem upon which to construct a healthy, happy life. Without it, some of the richest, most successful people in history might have lived lives of quiet desperation, wondering why their successes were never satisfying.

The goal is to communicate to your children that win or lose, pass or fail, you're glad to be their parents, and you'll be there for them. Stepchildren need this affirmation from their stepparents as well. A secure, nurturing parent or stepparent can meet this need for children. But accepting a child for who she is can be a problem in stepfamilies where insecure or immature stepparents struggle with their own self-esteem. Their stepchildren will sense that lack of acceptance and, in response, they may try too hard to please, or they may reject the stepparent. As a new stepparent, make acceptance a priority with your stepchildren.

Let your child know that while you admire his successes and share disappointment in his failures, you love him for himself.

By focusing on the following three areas, parents and stepparents will lay a solid foundation for valuing the children in their lives.

Separate worth from accomplishments. A child's worth is less a matter of what he does and more a matter of who he is. Let your child know that while you admire his successes and share disappointment in his failures, you love him for himself.

> *"Playing your hardest is more important than winning."*

> *"Losing doesn't make a person a loser."*

Separate worth from misbehavior. Just as a child's worth **isn't** the sum total of her accomplishments, nor is she the sum of her misbehaviors. A useful way to approach this is with the attitude that there are no bad children, only bad behavior. If a child is labeled "bad," she may eventually come to believe the label as truth. Along the same lines, mistakes aren't indications of a lack of worth; they're a natural and important part of growth and development. Children (and adults) who are afraid of being imperfect actually retard their own growth and development. Strive to help them learn to make friends with their mistakes.

"When I get angry at you, it doesn't mean I don't like you. It means that I don't like something you've done."

"Now that you've made that mistake, you know what not to do. You're one step closer to success!"

Appreciate each child's uniqueness. Although it's important to teach children that all people are equal, that doesn't mean all people are the same. It's encouraging for your child or stepchild to know that she's one of a kind. Appreciate her uniqueness by taking an interest in her activities and learning more about her. Be sure to say and do things that show the child that you like her for her unique self.

"This room really reflects you! I could never have decorated it for you."

"You're the only you in the whole world. I'm so glad that you're my stepdaughter!"

"I really appreciate you."

Stepfamily Enrichment Activity: Letter of Encouragement

Here's a true story from Michael Popkin:

As a young Sunday School teacher, I became annoyed with the idea of having to give grades to my students. Grades seemed an inadequate way to express either their progress or the way I felt about them after sharing nine months together. I decided to write each of my students a personal letter to go with the grades. While writing the letters, I found myself describing the positive aspects of each child and how he or she was progressing. These "letters of encouragement" were received appreciatively as the children left for summer vacation.

I didn't think much more about the letters until four years later. I was at a reception when a woman approached me and introduced herself as the mother of one of my students from that same Sunday School class. "That letter you wrote Alice meant so much to her," she said. "You know, she still has it on her bulletin board."

Somehow, "putting it in writing" carries that extra weight that makes it special.

All of the encouragement skills discussed in this session could be considered stepfamily enrichment activities, but somehow, "putting it in writing" carries that extra weight that makes it special. In addition, the child can refer to a letter of encouragement in the future and rekindle the warm feeling it generated, just as Alice did. This week's activity is to write a letter of encouragement to each of your children and stepchildren. Let your letter have the following characteristics.

- Write about the child's improvement in some area—not necessarily perfection, though.

- Write only truthful statements; don't say that the child has improved when he really hasn't.

- Be specific about what the improvements are.

- Write how the child's behavior has been helpful to others.

A sample letter might look like this:

Dear Brenda,

You know how frustrated we get with each other sometimes! It seems it's been too easy for me to tell you what's wrong and harder for me to tell you how much I see you doing right—or what a neat kid you are.

So I want to tell you why I feel so lucky to have you as my step-daughter. I admire so many of your traits. You're an achiever, whether you're playing your trumpet or hiking a mountain trail. You always try to do your best, but mostly I really like your attitude when you don't win. You're assertive—even when some risks you've taken were unpopular with your friends. That takes courage, girl, and you have it. You're responsible. You keep up your schoolwork, do school activities and your music, and still manage to help out around the house. I really appreciate that.

If I could have had a daughter of my own, I would have wanted her to be just like you. Please don't forget that—ever!

Love,

Mom II

Marriage Enrichment Activity: Encouraging Each Other

Couples thrive on encouragement just as your children do. It's important to value your partner for being who he is, just as it's essential to do this for your children.

In the midst of your complicated and often chaotic stepfamily, it's a real challenge to show your partner appreciation and encouragement, much less keep romance alive. But couples thrive on encouragement just as your children do. It's important to value your partner for being who he is, just as it's essential to do this for your children. Do you remember why you fell in love with your partner in the first place? Date nights and holidays away from the kids are great, but ultimately it's the everyday, thoughtful things that matter and keep romance alive.

It's important to let your partner know that you appreciate these "little things" and that they aren't going unnoticed. Over a cup of tea or glass of wine, agree to do the following exercise together. The goal is for each of you to identify some things you do for each other that make you happy. Be specific and positive. As you write your list, consider completing this sentence: "I feel appreciated and loved by you when you. . ."

Here are some examples:

- *Listen to me without trying to fix things*

- *Bring me coffee in bed*

- *Give me the opinion page of the newspaper first*

- *Make Wednesday night suppers*

- *Compliment me for no reason at all*

- *Call just to say you love me with no strings, no errands*

- *Share what you're thinking about*

After you've written your lists, take time to share them with each other. Pause between each item on the list for your partner to really absorb your appreciation.

Next, think about some caring behaviors that you've always wanted from your partner but never asked for. They may be private wishes you've held inside or something you feared he might not like to do. Avoid making requests that are already a source of conflict. Again, make separate lists completing this sentence: "Something I'd love for you to consider doing for me is..."

- *Read to me aloud before bedtime*

- *Go to the theatre with me more often*

- *Try backpacking in the mountains with me*

- *Shower and brush your teeth before you come to bed rather than in the morning*

- *Create a "secret date" once a month*

Again, after you've created your lists, share them with one another. When your partner requests something that you don't think you can do, or feels hurtful, rather than becoming defensive, try this response. "Hmmmm, let me consider that one."

Family Meeting: Emphasizing Stepfamily Unity

We believe that families are the backbone of civilization and that your family is the most important in the world...to your children. This is true whether yours is a traditional family or a stepfamily. In both cases, the family unit serves the same purpose in society. History has proven time after time that alone we could never survive, but by forming small, cooperative units, we can thrive. To a large extent, the measure of any civilization rests on the strength of its families. In a society such as ours, in which a high divorce rate threatens the strength of families, stepfamilies have their work cut out for them. They work hard to bring individuals back together to form new building blocks of society.

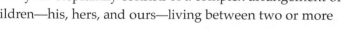

When your stepfamily consists of a complex arrangement of children—his, hers, and ours—living between two or more

Give your children the gift of memories by sharing the special stories of your families' histories—stories that are now part of your stepfamily's identity.

households, it can be quite a challenge to establish a sense of family unity, but it's important that you do. Look for ways to let your children know that they're part of a family unit: plan frequent family activities; use phrases like "in our family"; and develop your own traditions and rituals that combine elements of both family histories. Give your children the gift of memories by sharing the special stories of your families' histories—stories that are now part of your stepfamily's identity.

Take some time this week to gather your stepfamily together to talk about some aspect of the history of each family group, such as how that family came to live in this country or how grandparents met. Be sure to give equal time to each family group. You might even invite a grandparent or parent from the other household to participate. Share whatever special stories you can remember, and answer the children's questions with encouragement. If you don't know much about the histories connected to your stepfamily, consider making it a family project to find out. There's an abundance of family heritage information on the Internet, and your local library can help, too.

Remember also that through your stepfamily, your children will learn that they belong to a much larger family: the family of humankind. And since their contributions to that family will help determine the future of all people, your role as a parent or stepparent may very well be the most important job in the world.

Your Stepfamily Crest

Here's a simple and fun activity that you can add to your family meeting about unity. It's a great way for your stepfamily to work together as it forms its own unique identity.

Prepare family members for this activity by asking each of them to think about the symbols that best represent who they are (their beliefs, personal histories, hobbies, and favorite things) and symbols that represent your stepfamily (things you have in common, shared values, fond memories, favorite things to do together). Ask them to bring to the meeting a special token from an event you've already shared together as a family: shells from a beach trip, ticket stubs, photographs, or an autumn leaf from a hike together, for example.

When the time comes for your family to create its crest, here's how: cut a shield shape out of a large piece of cardboard and draw lines to divide the shield's space into sections. It should have a central space surrounded by smaller spaces—one for each family member. See the illustration for an idea of how a four-person family might divide the shield's space. Have each family member decorate his section to represent himself, using magazine cut-outs, photos, drawings, or whatever odds and ends he wishes to add. Then, decorate the central space to represent your stepfamily as a whole. Each family member should add the special token that he brought to the meeting. As each token is added, talk about the memories it elicits. Complete the central space by adding cut-outs, photos, etc. that have meaning to your family, and encourage more discussion of happy times together.

Another option for this activity is to create a family collage, where everyone contributes to filling the entire shield. There are no rules except to be creative, have fun, and ponder your stepfamily's identity.

Summing It Up

- Use the FLAC Method (feelings, limits, alternatives, consequences) to defuse power struggles in your stepfamily.

- Parents should model how to use anger positively for their children.

- Recognize that you might be discouraging your children, and learn to stop doing it.

- Encourage your children as much as possible: stimulate their independence; build on their strengths; show confidence in them; and value them as they are.

- Courage motivates positive risk-taking.

- Nudge children towards independence by allowing them to make some mistakes and learn to solve problems for themselves.

- Encouragement is necessary for a strong couple relationship.

- A letter of encouragement from a parent or stepparent makes a powerful and positive statement to a child.

- Sharing and preserving your stepfamily's history can strengthen your relationships and help form a sense of stepfamily unity.

Chapter 5

HOME ACTIVITIES

- Practice using the **FLAC Method** to prevent or handle a power struggle. Do the guide sheet on page 198.

- Practice all the different types of encouragement on your children (stimulating independence, building on strengths, showing confidence, and valuing your children) and do the guide sheets on pages 199-202.

- For your Stepfamily Enrichment Activity, write and give each of your children and stepchildren a letter of encouragement. Complete the guide sheet on page 203.

- Enrich your couple relationship by encouraging each other. Share your lists of things you appreciate about your partner and things you'd like your partner to try.

- Hold a Family Meeting to talk about your stepfamily's multiple histories and to build a sense of family unity. Use this time to make a stepfamily crest together.

Using the FLAC Method to Defuse Power Struggles

Look for an opportunity to use the FLAC method to reduce or avoid a power struggle at home this week. Then evaluate how it went by answering the questions below.

1. Who was the power struggle with, and what was it about? _____
   _____
   _____

2. What was the child **F**EELING, and how did you respond to these feelings? _____
   _____
   _____

3. What **L**IMITS did you remind your child about? _____
   _____
   _____

4. What **A**LTERNATIVES did you and your child discuss for helping him meet his needs within
   those limits? _____
   _____
   _____

5. Did you need to use any logical **C**ONSEQUENCES to help your child stay within the limits? If
   so, what were they? _____
   _____
   _____

6. What went well with the process? _____
   _____
   _____

7. What changes will you make next time? _____
   _____
   _____

Encouragement: Stimulating Independence

Think of things that you are now doing for your children and stepchildren that they could be doing for themselves. For example, making their beds, picking up their clothes, cleaning up after them. Make a list below:

1. _____

2. _____

3. _____

4. _____

5. _____

6. _____

7. _____

8. _____

Now, choose one of these to let each child do for him- or herself this week. Be sure to be encouraging as you turn this over to each child, and practice our encouragement skills as each child progresses.

Afterwards . . .

What did you like about how it went? _____

_____

_____

_____

What can you do to improve things next time?_____

_____

_____

_____

Encouragement: Building on Strengths

Identify a goal you have for one of your children or stepchildren. Then, use the four steps described on pages **183-184** to encourage your child's progress towards that goal.

Your goal: _____

Baby steps. Break the process of achieving the goal into five small steps, and write them below.

1. _____
2. _____
3. _____
4. _____
5. _____

Acknowledge what your child already does well. Write down three steps that your child has already mastered or strengths that will help your child achieve the goal:

1. _____
2. _____
3. _____

Next, talk with your child about the goal and acknowledge these strengths in the conversation. How did the talk go?

_____

Did you get your child's agreement to work on the goal together? If not, how will you approach your child differently next time? _____

_____

If your child agreed to work on the goal, fill in the final two steps after working together:

Nudge your child to take the next step. How did you encourage your child to take the next step? How did it go, and what might you do differently next time? _____

_____

Keep encouraging improvement and persistence (especially after backsliding) until the goal has been met. What words or actions did you find were encouraging to your child? _____

_____

Encouragement: Showing Confidence

Find ways to encourage your child by showing confidence in one or more of the four ways described below. Then, complete the questions for the method(s) you chose.

1. What **responsibility** did you give your child? _____

_____

How did he or she handle it? _____

_____

How can you improve the situation? _____

_____

2. What did you **ask your child's advice** about? _____

_____

How did he or she respond? _____

_____

3. When did you **avoid the temptation to take over** for your child? _____

_____

How did you encourage your child to stick with it? _____

_____

How did he or she respond? _____

_____

4. When did you **show that you expected success or positive behavior**? _____

_____

How did he or she respond? _____

_____

What did you do to follow up? _____

_____

Encouragement: Valuing Your Child

Find ways to show that you value your child or stepchild for who he is, using some of the methods detailed on pages **187-189**. Then, complete the questions for the method(s) you chose.

1. How did you **separate worth from accomplishments**? _____

_____

How did your child respond? _____

_____

What would you do the same or differently next time? _____

_____

2. How did you **separate worth from misbehavior**? _____

_____

How did your child respond? _____

_____

What would you do the same or differently next time? _____

_____

3. How did you show that you **appreciate your child's uniqueness**? _____

_____

How did your child respond? _____

_____

What would you do the same or differently next time? _____

_____

4. What special **words and actions** did you use to let your child know that you value him just for himself—unconditionally? _____

_____

How did your child respond? _____

_____

What would you do the same or different next time? _____

_____

Letter of Encouragement

Remember when ...

Recall a time from your childhood when one of your parents said or did something that you found encouraging. Take a moment to visualize the experience and to rekindle the positive feeling it provided.

What did your parent do or say? _____

How did you feel? _____

Now, try to find a letter or note that you found encouraging, from your parents or someone else.

What encouraged you about it? _____

Use this space to write a rough draft of a letter of encouragement to one of your children. Then copy the letter onto stationery or other paper before placing it where your child will find it—or mailing it!

_____
_____
_____
_____
_____
_____
_____
_____
_____
_____
_____
_____
_____

The secret to your stepfamily's success is both simple and complex. You've learned the wisdom of taking whatever time is necessary to navigate the often bumpy and twisting path towards stepfamily success with a positive "I know we can do this" attitude. The simple part is in understanding that this is a process and you must patiently work through its stages; the complex part is actually doing it! Time and process. Process and time. Remaining aware of these two critical factors will give you the patience and perspective you need to make it through the tough times, eventually leading you to a place where you can celebrate your hard-won stepfamily success. With that success comes a bonus: a feeling of great pride as you reap the rewards of a job well done.

A Conscious Commitment

The high divorce rate among remarried couples suggests that not everyone has the necessary staying power to make it through the challenges of stepfamily living. Because developing a satisfying stepfamily is a process that takes much time and patience, many of these couples probably gave up too soon or weren't prepared for what was ahead. There are times when most couples feel like giving up, but what separates those who eventually succeed from those who don't is often a matter of commitment. If you're going to be one of the success stories, it's essential that you make a long-term commitment to building your new stepfamily. Can you make the following statement with conviction?

> *"I am committed to the success of this stepfamily,*
> *through the good times and the bad."*

Say it to yourself, to your partner (and get your partner to say it, too!), in a family meeting, to your in-laws. The more people you tell about your commitment, the more invested you'll be in making it happen. Of course, the challenge is moving beyond words and into action, but if you're committed, you won't be quick to consider the option of quitting.

Societies all over the world place a high value on perseverance and positive thinking, and for a good reason: belief in them makes things happen! Recall the children's story, "The Little Engine That Could," a long-time favorite tale about a little locomotive who was heavily laden and had to cross a high mountain. He feared that he might not be able to make it up the very steep grade, and he began to have serious self-doubts. But a part of him believed that he just might be able to do it and that he shouldn't give up. He re-created his thinking into a positive mantra: *I think I can. I think I can.* That's the same kind of positive thinking you'll need to succeed in your remarriage. Like that little engine who made it up the mountain and down the other side, turn your belief about making your stepfamily successful into an affirmation that you repeat to yourself during hard times. Against all odds, and simply because he believed he could do it, the little train succeeded and, afterwards, he felt a great sense of pride in his achievement—as will you!

Don't Give Up! Trust the Process.

Perhaps you've made mistakes in your new stepfamily. After all, everybody does. If you made the mistake of not preparing adequately for the transition to stepfamily living, you might find yourself bogged down in a mire of problems early on. For example, one mistake couples often make is to believe in the fantasy that new love can overcome all obstacles. But you'll soon find that love cannot conquer all, or at least it can't conquer all of the complex challenges that your new family will face. If this is where you find yourself today, don't give up! If unforeseen experiences or problematic relationships have taken your stepfamily on a different course than you expected, don't give up! Even if you've had an exceptionally rough time, it doesn't mean you're failing, only that your stepfamily has experienced some setbacks and specific challenges. Still, you can manifest your hopes and dreams.

To succeed, you need good information about stepfamily living; you need skills and tools; you need the support of others; and you need an ample dose of reality. Now that you've nearly completed this program, you have the education, tools, and skills you need to succeed. If, after taking this class, you become aware that you have more serious issues to resolve with your partner or members of your stepfamily, seek out a marriage and family therapist who's had special training in stepfamily dynamics and who teaches skills. Check the resource guide at the end of this book for suggestions about where to get that help. When you make a conscious commitment to the success of your stepfamily and learn to trust in the slow but sure process of becoming a different kind of family, you can begin transforming stressful relationships into special ones. The caring and concern that comes from facing reality through teamwork will lead you to toward the success you seek. And when it happens, you can begin to celebrate!

The caring and concern that comes from facing reality through teamwork will lead you to toward the success you seek.

But before the celebrating begins, let's return to a very important and serious topic that has come up time and time again in this book: your role in keeping your children safe. By now, you should be familiar with the idea that children in stepfamilies, because of their history of loss and change, may be more likely than other children to engage in risky behavior. Part of the problem is that these kids are also more likely to lack the parental support they need during this painful time of transition, and so some may fall through the cracks of the stepfamily's two (or more)-household system. By taking an active role in your children's lives and not allowing them to "fall through the cracks," you can make all the difference.

Parenting as Prevention: Drugs, Sexuality, and Violence

There had been a lot of drinking at the party, including a keg of beer that poured freely. Many of the teens were busily getting drunk in the front yard when a carload of uninvited guests arrived. These teens were from another high school and had also been drinking. They arrived angry that one of their girlfriends had come to the party with a boy from the other school. Harsh words quickly escalated into a fight with as many as twenty teenagers joining in. The noise got the attention of the party host's parents, who had been keeping to themselves upstairs. But before the adults could intervene or get help, one of the kids pulled out a knife and stabbed another boy in the stomach. After a panic-stricken call to 911, an ambulance arrived to rush the victim to the hospital. But the injury was serious, and the boy died in the emergency room. His death sent shockwaves through the entire community.

While it may be true that too many parents leave their teenagers unattended at home, allowing them to engage in wild and risky behavior, this story points out that there's more to protecting your children than simply being there. In this case, the parents were home. Upstairs. Watching TV. When asked later why they hadn't been downstairs supervising the party, they replied, "because we didn't want to get in the way."

Developing Protective Factors

We believe it's the responsibility of parents and stepparents to get in the way.

The Center for Substance Abuse and Prevention (CSAP) has identified numerous protective factors that exist in six different domains, or life areas. Research shows that the more of these protective factors that exist in a child's life, the less likely the child is to experiment with or become negatively involved with alcohol, tobacco, or other drugs (ATODs).

The chart on the next two pages details these protective factors by domain, and also presents ways that parents can help develop these factors in their children. The most obvious domain that parents can influence is the Family domain. However, as the chart shows, there are many ways that we can develop protective factors in the other domains as well. Please read over this chart carefully, and ask yourself the following questions:

- *How many of these actions am I already taking to develop these protective factors in my children or stepchildren?*

- *How many of these actions could I start taking?*

- *What skills do I need to learn or practice in order to be more effective in developing these factors in my children or stepchildren? (Chapter references are provided to review skills taught in this guide that will help you.)*

Protective Factor	How parents can help develop them
INDIVIDUAL DOMAIN	

Positive personal characteristics, including: social skills and social responsiveness; cooperativeness; emotional stability, positive sense of self; flexibility; problem-solving skills; and low levels of defensiveness

Bonding to societal institutions and values, including: attachment to parents and extended family; commitment to school; regular involvement with religious institutions; and belief in society's values

Social and emotional competence, including: good communication skills, responsiveness; empathy; caring; sense of humor, inclination toward prosocial behavior; problem-solving skills; sense of autonomy; sense of purpose and of the future (e.g., goal-directedness); and self-discipline

- Work to instill qualities of good character in child (i.e. courage, character, self-esteem, and respect). *(Chapters 1 and 5)*
- Encourage positive bonding with child. *(Stepfamily Enrichment Activities, All Chapters)*
- Communicate expectations clearly, and listen actively. *(Chapter 2)*
- Provide child with age-appropriate choices. *(Method of Choice: Chapter 1)*
- Help child solve problems he owns, and involve child in solving family problems. *(Chapters 2 and 4)*
- Build on child's strengths, and show confidence in child's ability. *(Chapter 5)*
- Help child manage anger. *(Chapter 4)*

FAMILY DOMAIN	

Positive bonding among family members

Parenting that includes: high levels of warmth and avoidance of severe criticism; sense of basic trust; high parental expectations; and clear and consistent expectations, including children's participation in family decisions and responsibilities.

An emotionally supportive parental/family milieu, including: parental attention to children's interests; orderly and structured parent-child relationships; and parent involvement in homework and school-related activities

- Express love and affection to child on a regular basis. Establish routines and be consistent with them. *(Chapters 2 and 5)*
- Use positive discipline methods. *(Chapters 4 and 5)*
- Emphasize family unit. *(Stepfamily Enrichment Activities, all Chapters)*
- Involve child in family decisions and responsibilities. *(Family Meetings, All Chapters; Problem Prevention Talks, Chapter 4)*
- Encourage child in all areas, including school, and build on child's strengths. *(Chapter 5)*
- Value child for who he or she is. *(Chapter 5)*
- Communicate expectations clearly. *(Chapters 1 and 2)*

Continued on Next Page

Protective Factor	How parents can help develop them
PEER DOMAIN	
Association with peers who are involved in school, recreation, service, religion, or other organized activities	• Encourage positive peer relationships. • Expose child to opportunities to form positive peer relationships. *(Chapters 5 and 6)*
SCHOOL DOMAIN	
Caring and support; sense of "community" in classroom and school High expectations from school personnel Clear standards and rules for appropriate behavior Youth participation, involvement, and responsibility in school tasks and decisions	• Be involved in school activities. • Be informed of what is happening in your child's school. • Know your child's teachers, and attend parent-teacher conferences. • Show your child that learning and school are a priority. • Read with your child regularly. • Encourage your child in schoolwork/learning. *(Chapter 5)* • Build on child's strengths, and show confidence in child's ability. *(Chapter 5)*
COMMUNITY DOMAIN	
Caring and support High expectations of youth Opportunities for youth participation in community activities	• Seek out and provide opportunities for child to participate in positive community activities • Provide other adult mentors in your child's life *(Chapter 6)*
Protective Factor	How parents can help develop them
SOCIETY DOMAIN	
Media literacy (resistance to pro-use messages) Decreased accessibility Increased pricing through taxation Raised purchasing age and enforcement Stricter driving-while-under-the-influence laws	• Monitor child's exposure to media. (TV, Internet, magazines, books, etc.) • Provide child with positive media exposure and limit negative exposure. • Discuss issues brought up in the media with child, especially regarding alcohol, tobacco, other drugs. Listen actively to his point of view, and share yours convincingly. *(Chapter 2)* • Limit child's exposure to alcohol, tobacco, and other drugs. *(Chapter 6)*

Based on the CSAP (Center for Substance Abuse and Prevention) model of Protective Factors for youth prevention. This and other related information is published at www.samhsa.gov/centers/csap/csap.html

Getting in the Way: Parents Filtering Events

One purpose of this program is to help you instill qualities of character in your children, whether they are your biological children or your stepchildren. Building character will enable them to make good decisions when events start getting out of hand. We've talked about handling problems in ways that move children into success cycles so that they can use their best thinking, feeling, and doing to meet such challenges. We've talked about the importance of not overprotecting kids, but allowing them to learn from the natural consequences of their actions as they develop into independent adults.

Even so, there are still times when parents and stepparents should GET IN THE WAY! The technical term for this is *interdiction*, and it's no accident that it's often applied to the drug trade, as in "drug enforcement agents interdicted illegal drugs coming into the country." Just as governments try to filter out illegal drugs before they get into the system, active parents and stepparents use their presence as filters to prevent dangerous events from influencing the children in their charge.

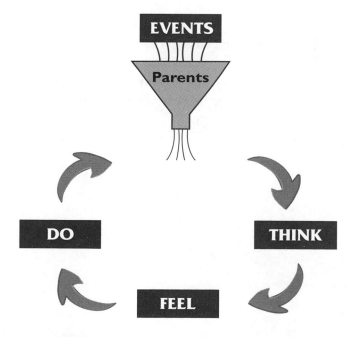

As the graphic shows, parents and stepparents can sometimes come between their children and the events that affect them, filtering the events' influence over the child's think-feel-do cycle. These events should include those that are excessively dangerous, such as an unsupervised party with underage drinking for the teens in the earlier example. You are probably already tuned into many of these risks for younger children.

Examples of Excessively Dangerous Events

One type of excessively dangerous events includes physical risks such as:

- *Climbing too high or swimming without supervision*

- *Riding without seatbelts or in unsafe vehicles*

- *Being left unsupervised in public places*

- *Being left around known bullies or other violent people*

- *Playing in a busy street or other unsafe place*

- *Being near poisons or other dangerous household objects*

The second type of risk that parents and stepparents should strive to filter out as much as possible includes events that are likely to have a negative influence on a child's development of beliefs, attitudes, values, and character. You should be particularly vigilant about influences that might encourage the use of tobacco, alcohol or other drugs, reckless sexuality, and violence

Examples of Negative Influences

Unrestricted use of media. This can include the Internet, TV, movies, music, books, magazines, and games. The following tips can help:

- *Read rating systems and use them*

- *Don't cave in and allow kids to view more mature material than they're ready for. Make sure you've viewed it first if you plan to make an exception to the rating guide.*

- *View, play, or listen to what your children are doing from time to time to stay on top of what messages are being communicated. Then, don't be afraid to limit those that are too sexual, violent, or otherwise run counter to your values. Discuss your reasons with the children and listen actively to theirs. But, as their guardian, the final call is yours to make.*

- *Keep TVs and computers in public living areas of your home so that you can easily check what's being viewed.*

- *Watch some TV shows with your children and stepchildren and, at times, use other media with them so you can discuss important themes that come up.*

- *Learn to use parental controls provided by Internet providers and other methods of monitoring what your child is watching.*

- *Talk with the parents of your children's friends and encourage them to be vigilant also. Kids often seek out homes where the restrictions are lax, so support each other.*

Peers and other friends who are known to break rules, encourage misbehavior, and even break laws. This is tricky because you don't want to dictate who your children's friends can be, which may lead to rebellion and sneaking. Avoid judging on the basis of looks alone. However, let each child in your family know that if she and another child get into trouble together, then they must not be having a good influence on each other. The logical consequence is to keep them from seeing each other (outside of school) or to require an adult to monitor them for a time. Allow them to try again after a reasonable period—if they still want to.

Adults whose values differ greatly from your own, even including adult friends, teachers, and clergy. While exposure to other people's ideas is healthy for children, you can reasonably attempt to limit your child from being around adults who display values that are radically different from your own family values. Choose schools, religious institutions, and other places that support your values. Be sure that you and your partner agree about the values you want to emphasize.

When you cannot limit these influences, be sure to talk with your children about what they are exposed to in a way that presents your viewpoint. For example,

> *"I know Aunt Cathy smokes, and she's a cool lady in a lot of ways, but smoking is a terrible thing for her to do to herself for all the reasons we've talked about."*

Getting In the Way: Encouraging Positive Events

If parents and stepparents can filter OUT certain negative events that might harm or negatively influence children, they can also filter IN, or encourage, positive events that can help build character that leads to a success cycle. As much as people might like to think otherwise, no child gets everything he needs from his parents. Kids have to supplement what you give them with influences from other adults and peers. Parents can help this process along by thinking of creative ways to provide encouraging influences on their children's development. For example:

Positive adult influences. Make sure that the children in your family have positive contact with other adult mentors, such as:

- *Spiritual youth group leaders*

- *Teachers and sports coaches*

- *Adult friends*

- *Relatives, especially grandparents and others without young children of their own*

- *Mentoring programs such as Big Brothers/Big Sisters.*

Media. There are many positive role models and lessons in books, movies, music, TV, and the Internet. Help your children find and take advantage of this positive input, and you'll strengthen many positive values.

Summer camp. Camp counselors and other staff can be a wonderful influence on children's development. This gives kids a chance to develop their skills and character away from home as they become exposed to many new and positive influences.

A loving, spiritual education. When delivered in a loving and supportive manner, a spiritual education will provide many positive lessons of character as well as faith.

A good academic environment. Let's face it— all schools aren't created equal. Your children will spend more time at school than any other place (other than their beds), so find the best one that your financial situation will allow, even if it means moving. The value of a good educational environment is more than just the teachers and facilities. Just as important is the quality of the other kids and families that your child goes to school and plays with, as they will also influence your child.

Holding Character Talks

Building positive values and character in your children and stepchildren is a matter of using many of the skills in this book—from disciplining behavior that promotes negative values to encouraging behavior that supports positive ones. You can do this in little ways in your daily interactions with your children, and through the examples you set through your own words and actions. But the notion that "values are caught, not taught" is only half true. Group discussion can be a very effective way to teach values.

This chapter's family meeting is to discuss your family's values regarding drugs, sexuality, and violence. This is an opportunity for you to use your persuasive skills to back up your rules and discipline. After all, it's one thing to set limits; it's another to win the minds of your children. If you can give them reasons that make sense to them for your rules, you'll equip your kids with one of the best prevention tools available: positive values. The following tips will help you get this talk off to a good start:

1. **Introduce the topic.** Starting a group discussion is often the most difficult part. It's helpful to plan how you'll introduce the subject. A simple introduction for your first talk might go something like this:

   We called this meeting because we want to take time now and then to talk about topics that are important to all of us—topics that have to do with the kind of people we're becoming. And I say "we" because your parents are still growing and changing, too. The topic we've chosen for our first talk is "tobacco, alcohol, and other drugs."

   Different family members might choose topics for future talks, and each might prepare his own introduction.

2. **Ask open-ended questions.** Once you've introduced the topic, having a few good questions prepared can help launch the discussion. Consider these ahead of time, making sure that they're open-ended. This means that they cannot be answered with a simple "yes" or "no." For example,

   Closed questions:

   "Do you think staying away from illegal drugs is important"?

   Open-ended questions:

   "What are some ways that tobacco, alcohol, and other drugs hurt people?"

   "What are some examples of people you've seen or heard about who have been hurt by using them?"

   "Why does it sometimes take courage to avoid using them?"

   "What are some other reasons for avoiding these substances?"

3. **Listen and respond with empathy as you discuss the topic together.**
   Remember to use your active communication skills from Chapter Two and listen with empathy to your children's thoughts and feelings. This helps them develop their own emotional intelligence and encourages them to continue talking. Avoid communication blocks as you keep an open, nonjudgmental attitude about their thoughts and feelings. This is particularly important (and difficult) when they say something that goes against your own value system. However, if you're quick to judge or criticize (even nonverbally, with a disapproving facial expression), you run the risk of shutting down communication and limiting your chance to influence them. Here are some examples of how to respond with empathy:

   "That's an interesting point. I hadn't thought of that."

   "You must have been frightened when that happened, and yet you didn't go along just to fit in."

   "I'm not sure I agree with you about that, but it gives me another way to look at it."

4. **Share your own values persuasively.** Children today are less likely to accept our values and beliefs just because we tell them to. Being a positive influence requires providing accurate information, displaying sound reasoning, and using persuasive arguments. Bringing in outside resources such as a relevant magazine article, a movie, or even a TV show can help lend weight to your point of view. Sometimes relating a personal experience can create a story in your child's mind that helps him learn an important lesson. The more relevant you can make your examples to your child's experience, the better chance you have of making an impact on his core beliefs and values.

   "I thought the kid in that movie showed a lot of courage by standing up to his friends who wanted him to use drugs with them."

   "A lot of people think that smoking won't hurt them, but did you know that one out of every three people who smoke will die from smoking-related illnesses? Plus, it makes your teeth yellow and your breath stink, and it ages your skin quickly."

"I knew some kids back in school who thought they could handle alcohol, but they wound up as alcoholics."

5. **End with a treat or a fun activity.** It's always a good idea to end any meeting on a positive note, so have a treat ready, or decide on something fun to do together—maybe even one of the following stepfamily celebration activities.

Celebrate!

Celebrations add joy and meaning to your life. You and your family need to celebrate every so often, whether you do it with play, with humor, with projects, with planned events, or in any number of other ways. Too often, families forget to celebrate beyond the swapping of greeting cards. At the end of this chapter, we'll suggest several important events in stepfamily life that deserve a time for celebration. Choose one or two of them to do with your family this week, and then look for opportunities over time to do some more.

The following activities are great ways to celebrate your stepfamily journey as you deepen the connections between family members. Choose one or two to try this week, then come back to others as you like.

Celebrations add joy and meaning to your life. Too often, families forget to celebrate beyond the swapping of greeting cards.

Celebrate Your Differences

As we discussed in Chapter 3, conflicts are bound to arise when you attempt to merge diverse ways of doing things. When your stepfamily first came together, you created an expanded family culture—one with different elements that each set of family members brought along. Ideas about everything might have been different, from the shape of your Sunday morning pancakes and what belongs in a salad, to dealing with discipline and attending religious services. One way wasn't necessarily right and the other wrong. They were merely different.

The differences in your stepfamily might be in the way you have fun: your family's idea of a great time is to pack up the sleeping bags and tent and head to the woods for a camping trip; the new members of your stepfamily prefer city life to roughing it in the woods. Or perhaps the differences are personality based: one side is known for having a sense of humor; the other is fairly serious-minded. You might even end up in a stepfamily with two different religions—say, Christian and Jewish. By accepting these differences rather than butting up against them, you strengthen the family as a whole. And as individuals, trying new things will enrich your lives by broadening your experiences.

The merging of two family cultures can become challenging when people don't take time to share and explain why they do certain things. Sometimes your differences are minor, but unless you share them, they remain a mystery and possibly a source of confusion and agitation to other family members. When you celebrate the differences, this blending of family cultures can be an enriching learning experience for all of you.

Activity: Try this simple discussion activity as a way of getting to know more about your differences. It allows members of your stepfamily to talk about how things were done in their other families and how they're currently done in the other parent's household. Everyone should agree to share similarities and differences without ridicule, criticism, or verbal judgments. The goal is to learn more about each other. You need no materials, just your best listening skills.

Here's what to do: have your whole stepfamily sit in a circle. Someone starts by sharing, for example, how the morning routine went in his old house and/or in his other biological parent's house. Who awoke him in the morning? Did he have to make his bed and straighten his room before leaving for school? Did he walk to school, ride the bus, or get a ride from a parent? What happened when he forgot lunch money or after-school sports equipment?

These "same and different" discussions can cover many categories: mealtimes and snacks, after-school time, chores and responsibilities, bedtime, TV watching, holidays, etc. Consider as many topics as you can, for this is an excellent way to get to know one another, as well as to discuss and plan how things will go in your new family.

Celebrate Lessons You've Learned

Living in a stepfamily can offer you many ways to learn valuable lessons—including some lessons that you might not have thought you needed to learn. Crises provide great learning opportunities!

When you use a crisis as an opportunity to examine what needs to be corrected in your stepfamily, you promote growth and change for everyone, and often you stabilize from the crisis more quickly.

It's commonly believed that the Chinese expression for the word "crisis" consists of two characters that translate as "danger" and another that means "opportunity."

Danger   Opportunity

There is beauty and wisdom in the idea that a crisis is born from the merging of danger and opportunity; however, scholars of the language would tell us that there's little truth behind this claim: the two symbols that mean "crisis" are only vaguely related in meaning to the concepts of danger and opportunity. The misinterpretation probably resulted from a combination of incomplete translation and wishful thinking. But there's a reason that this idea has caught on: the lesson it teaches rings true. It helps us to be able to believe there is something positive and purposeful in a crisis, where normally we see only the negative. When you use a crisis as an opportunity to examine what needs to be corrected in your stepfamily, you promote growth and change for everyone, and often you recover from the crisis more quickly. Here's an example from one parent:

> *When my stepdaughter got pregnant, you could say that she finally got the attention she wanted. But it was the wrong kind of attention, and it impacted her life—and that of our family—in a negative way. As my wife and I dealt with the crisis, we learned that she was still grieving her parents' divorce and feeling angry and jealous of the little time she spent with her father. When she sought out a boyfriend—someone who she hoped would care about her and provide emotional reassurance—she made some poor choices that left her in a vulnerable situation. But when her mother and I rose to the occasion, helped her find support resources, and showed that we were there by her side, the three of us grew closer. Now my stepdaughter knows we care about her. She shares with us her wishes about important decisions she has ahead and problems she needs to face.*

In the face of a crisis, this stepfamily made some major changes. As they examined some hard family issues, began to listen to one another, faced what they needed to do, and committed to changes that made a difference, this stepfamily took a big step forward. As a result, they became less fearful of changes and challenges because they discovered the important lessons that such challenges held.

Activity: The purpose of this activity is to look back on challenging times your stepfamily has had and identify the lesson learned. Divide a piece of paper down the middle. At the top left side, write *crisis*; on the top right, write *lesson*. Have each family member offer at least one such memory and write each in the "crisis" column. Then review the crises together, asking each person to share what lesson they learned from the experience. You'll find that your family learned a great deal from working through these crises, and this becomes a lesson for your children to carry into their lives: don't run from challenges; rather, confront them and learn.

Celebrate One Another's Accomplishments

Stepfamily living should be a joyful experience. You want the members of your family to look forward to a warm and happy home atmosphere and feel like "home is where I want to be." In a cooperative, supportive, and flexible stepfamily, active parents allow children to be as self-sufficient and independent as possible. Such an environment creates a climate in which new relationships grow and flourish, and in which individuals can participate in activities that give them pleasure and build self-esteem: chess club, scouts, a choral group, soccer team, theatre group. Through these activities, your children can achieve and accomplish things that strengthen their character and abilities.

One of the best ways to build self-esteem in your children and stepchildren is to celebrate their accomplishments.

One of the best ways to build self-esteem in your children and stepchildren is to celebrate their accomplishments. Rather than having trophies and awards gathering dust in a closet, why not consider devoting an entire wall to celebrating the achievements of your family members? A set of shelves would be a perfect place to show off this collection, and making this a permanent fixture in your home is sure to make family members feel special.

Activity: If you have a large stepfamily, choose a "Kid of the Month" as a way to get to know each child or stepchild in greater depth. In no way should this title have to be earned or achieved. This should be a celebration of each individual, just for being who she is—a right that belongs to every child! Your selection process can be random, alphabetical, or start with the oldest child and move down. You'll need a fairly large bulletin board, hung in a prominent spot with a "Kid of the Month" heading in colorful letters. Sort through albums together and let the child choose favorite photos to be displayed of her from infancy on (she may have to get some photos from her other household). Include samples of artwork or schoolwork. Ask the child to write a brief paragraph on one or two special memories, as well as some dreams for her future. Have a place on the bulletin board to display her favorites—movie, book, food, activity, game, etc. On a night when all family members can gather, make a special dinner of the child's own menu selections and celebrate her for being just who she is. Let her tell her life's story as she remembers it (and don't correct her—this is her perception. Later, you can correct facts if you think they really matter). Ask questions. Do a go-round of appreciations with each family member telling her one special thing they appreciate about her. To make it more festive, you could even add handmade gifts. Celebrate in a big way, letting each child know they are an important part of your stepfamily!

Celebrate Your Marriage

(Here's your marriage enrichment activity for this week!)

Your marriage is the foundation of your stepfamily, and its strength and stability is essential to your stepfamily's success. Your marriage has given you another chance at love and at building a joyful family life—the things that might have eluded you the first time around. Once you get down to the business of creating a strong marriage, your children and stepchildren will begin to observe. They'll see you master challenges. They'll see you work hard toward improving your relationship and your parenting skills. And they'll see you have fun with your partner and take time out for nurturing your relationship. They'll watch you make your marriage the primary relationship in the family, and from that your children will learn the power of a healthy marriage and the sense of security it can provide. All of this observing will teach them that marriage is serious business and in need of constant tending. Your strong, healthy marriage will model for them what they'll want when they form adult partnerships someday. This is one of the greatest gifts you can give the children in your stepfamily.

Activity: Plan a celebration trip to honor your marriage—a big trip just for the two of you. You deserve it! It could be a celebration of an anniversary—five years or ten—but make it very special. Start a file folder and collect brochures and clippings about possible places to go. Start saving money in a marriage celebration fund. Choose a date and go. Celebrate your remarriage!

Celebrate Your Strengths

It's absolutely critical to focus on the strengths that being in a stepfamily—*your* stepfamily—offers. It's easy to identify the problems and struggles, but when you focus on your positive attributes and strengths, you'll identify possibilities that you'd never thought of before. This approach changes your perspective and keeps hope alive for the whole family.

Many rewards come from living in a stepfamily—some short-term, most long-term.

Activity: After a family meal, when you're all still sitting together, pass out a stack of small note sheets and pencils. Have each family member identify one family strength that they appreciate, such as creativity, flexibility, and inclusiveness, and write it on one of the notes sheets. Have each person try to contribute at least three sheets. Then, gather the pile of strengths in the middle of the table and have family members take turns drawing one and reading it aloud. Talk about how each strength makes a difference for your family. Appreciate these strengths. Treasure them!

Celebrate Your Stepfamily's Success: The Big Event

Hurrah! You made it! Through bad times and good, your stepfamily has pushed on towards resolution of past loss, better relationships, and a more stable home environment. You may not have come all the way yet; after all, we have stressed that stepfamily living is an ongoing process. But now it's time to celebrate what you have accomplished so far! As a family, brainstorm what you think would be a great way to honor your efforts towards building a happy and strong stepfamily. It should be something exciting that will demonstrate to each of you the importance of what you achieved by in your stepfamily journey. Would it be a party? A trip to a national park or a foreign country? If you can imagine it, you can do it!

Sit together as a family with a huge piece of paper and a marker. As you begin to brainstorm as a group, let the kids take turns writing the ideas you generate. Without considering time or money, share ideas. No idea is too outrageous, and the only limitation is your imagination. Once you have a huge list of possibilities, begin to cross out ones that don't work for the entire family for practical or financial reasons. Take time to discuss why these are unsatisfactory and talk about the pros and cons of each idea before you cross one out. Stay encouraging when eliminating ideas. For example, rather than saying, "That's too expensive," you might say "I love this one, but we'd have to save money for about ten years to visit the pyramids!" Narrow the list to three ideas that are both spectacular and possible. Then choose, #3, #2, and finally, the winner—#1. You can do this activity over several family meetings as an ending to regular stepfamily business.

The next step is finding a way to make it happen. Choose different family members to plan the trip or event: a researcher, a finance planner, a scheduler of pet care, etc. Start a file folder with brochures, Internet articles, and ideas about the chosen destination or event. Planning and taking this trip could be the adventure of a lifetime for your stepfamily, so work very hard as a group to make it happen.

In Conclusion

Congratulations on completing this book. The time and energy you have taken to complete this program testify to your commitment as a parent. You may have other jobs in your life, but none are more important than the work you do as a parent. Meeting the challenge of stepfamily living means more than just creating a pleasant place for all of you to live. It means helping to develop children who have the character and skills to move society forward. One of America's greatest presidents, Abraham Lincoln, grew up in a stepfamily after his mother died when he was only seven. His stepmother, who had three other children, was a loving and positive influence on the future president who wrote the following words:

> A child is a person who is going to carry on what you have started.
>
> He is going to sit where you are sitting, and when you are gone,
>
> Attend to those things which you think are important.
>
> You may adopt all the policies you please, but how they are carried out depends on him.
>
> He will assume control of your cities, states, and nations.
>
> He is going to move in and take over your churches, schools, universities, and corporations.
>
> All your books are going to be judged, praised, or condemned by him.
>
> The fate of humanity is in his hands.
>
> *-Abraham Lincoln*

People who live in successful stepfamilies eventually speak of the closeness they share because they worked through the challenges together. Most admit it wasn't easy—especially the "getting started" part. The process is slow, but the rewards are great: a home where differences are celebrated; where problems still exist but don't take over; where healing can happen; where sometimes love grows... not always, but that's all right. Respect, trust, and acceptance of one another are just as important as love; indeed, they are part of it. And where there is respect, trust, and acceptance, most things are possible.

Here's to you, your stepfamily, and your success!

Summing It Up

- It's important that you make a conscious commitment in order for your stepfamily to succeed.

- Don't give up when times get tough. Trust the process, and seek outside help if necessary.

- It's the job of parents and stepparents to "get in the way"! Learn to act as a filter for your kids: filter out the negative influences and filter in the positive influences.

- Celebrate the progress your stepfamily has made every step of the way.

Chapter 6

HOME ACTIVITIES

- **Hold a character talk with your child or children about alcohol, tobaco, and other drugs. Complete the guide sheet on page 228.**

- **Plan a celebration with your stepfamily. Use the ideas in this guide to get started.**

- **Review what you've learned by completing the crossword puzzle on page 229.**

Character Talk

Alcohol, Tobacco, and Other Drugs

Have a character talk about alcohold, tobacco, and other drugs with your family this week and answer the following questions.

Before the talk...

How will you introduce the topic? _____

_____

_____

What are some points that you want to be sure to make during the talk? _____

_____

_____

_____

What are some open-ended questions that you can use to stimulate discussion? _____

_____

_____

_____

What outside resources such as articles, a story or video will you use to help you be more persuasive? _____

_____

After the talk...

What were some things that you liked about how the talk went? _____

_____

_____

How did you listen with empathy as you discussed the topic together? _____

_____

What will you do differently next time to make it better? _____

_____

Crossword Puzzle

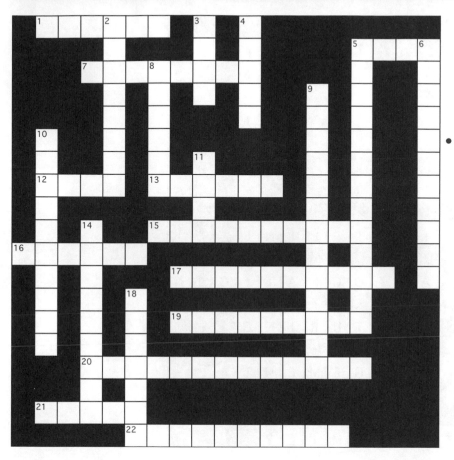

© 2006 Elizabeth Einstein and Steve Weyer

ACROSS

1 Rather than block communication, use __ _____communication to help your child solve a problem.

5 Acronym for method of defusing power struggles

7 Mad, sad, glad, and scared are examples of _____.

12 A stepparent seeks an effective and comfortable _____ in the stepfamily.

13 Use logical consequences instead of punishment and _____.

15 From the Latin meaning "to teach": One of the greatest stepfamily challenges

16 Gives power to kids and helps prevent power struggles

17 "Dictator" style of parenting

19 Best way to build trust with a new stepchild

20 Best way to build confidence & motivate children

21 Unfounded beliefs about stepfamily living

22 A type of family faced with many challenges and great possibilities

DOWN

2 Powerful discipline / communication tool used to eliminate blame

3 New stepparents must work hard to build a _____ with each stepchild.

4 Use of drugs, sex & violence are examples of teenage_____

5 Family gathering to solve problems & make plans

6 Two or more people working together in a mutually supportive manner for a common good

8 A child is a learner, a parent is a_____

9 Most effective parenting style

10 Activities that enhance family unity and bonds

11 In the "problem handling model," the key is who ____the problem

14 The stepfamily is___ from the traditional family in its structure & development

18 Building a successful stepfamily involves trusting the _____

229

Crossword Puzzle Solution

Resource Guide

To Find Outside Help

American Association for Marriage and Family Therapy
www.aamft.org
A professional association for the field of marriage and family therapy. Web site includes a "Therapist Locator" where you can seek a highly-trained family systems expert in your area.

National Stepfamily Resource Center
www.stepfamilies.info
Formerly the Stepfamily Association of America, this comprehensive resource center helps you locate information on programs, services, research, law and policy, and therapists who have been trained specifically in stepfamily education.

Stepfamilies

Bonus Families
www.bonusfamilies.com
International organization dedicated to supporting stepfamilies and promoting peaceful coexistence between divorced or separated parents and their new families.

Our Family Wizard
www.ourfamilywizard.com
A subscription-based web tool to assist separated family members with scheduling and communication. Includes online calendars, message board, expense management, and more.

Stepfamily InFormation
www.sfhelp.org
Comprehensive source for stepfamily information from stepfamily expert Peter Gerlach.

Stepfamily Living
www.stepfamilyliving.com
Elizabeth Einstein's official web site. Go here for more information about her publications, workshops, and counseling services.

Single Parenting

Parents Without Partners
www.parentswithoutpartners.org
Provides single parents and their children with opportunities for enhancing personal growth by offering an environment for support, friendship and the exchange of parenting techniques.

Marriage and Families

Coalition for Marriage, Family, and Couples Education (CMFCE)
www.smartmarriages.com
An information exchange to help couples locate marriage and relationship education resources. Offers an annual "Smart Marriages, Happy Families" conference.

National Center for Fathering
www.fathers.com
An online resource for everyday dads created by the National Center for Fathering. Site provides research-based training, practical tips and resources to help men be the involved fathers, grandfathers, and father figures their children need.

Divorce

Children's Rights Council
www.crckids.org
A child-advocacy organization serving divorced, never-married and extended families, and at-risk youth.

Divorce Support
www.divorcesupport.com
Everything you need to know before, during, and after a divorce, including state-by-state legal information, support forums, and parenting guidance.

Earthquake in Zipland
www.ziplandinteractive.com
A creative, interactive computer game with dialogue, adventure, and intrigue designed to help kids cope with the loss and intense emotion associated with parents' separation and divorce.

Further Reading

These books are distributed by Active Parenting. Call 800.825.0060 or visit www.activeparenting.com to order.

35 Ways to Help a Grieving Child
from the Dougy Center for Grieving Children
Item #T8689

Changing Family Games
by Beth Marcozzi
Item #T7086

Ex-Etiquette for Parents: Good Behavior After a Divorce or Separation
by Jann Blackstone-Ford, MA and Sharyl Jupe
Item #T8708

Jessica's Two Families
by Lynn Hugo, illustrated by Adam Gordon
Item #T8832

Jigsaw Puzzle Family: The Stepkids' Guide to Fitting It Together
by Cynthia MacGregor
Item #T8792

Remarried with Children: 10 Secrets for Successfully Blending and Extending Your Family
by Barbara LeBey
Item # T8703

Stay Close: 40 Clever Ways to Connect with Kids When You're Apart
by Tenessa Gemelke
Item # 8806

Stepparenting: Everything You Need to Know to Make It Work
by Jeannette Lofas
Item #T8651

Strengthening Your Stepfamily
By Elizabeth Einstein, MA, LMFT, and Linda Albert, PhD
Item #T8726

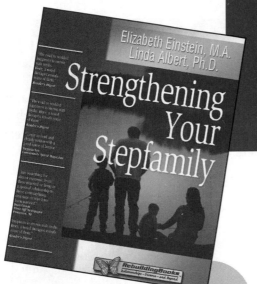

Strengthening Your Stepfamily

New Roles and Relationships for Couples, Parents and Children

by Elizabeth Einstein, MA, LMFT, and Linda Albert, PhD

Strengthening Your Stepfamily
Softcover, 261 pages, $17.95
ISBN 1-886230-62-5
Available from Active Parenting Publishers, your local bookseller, and other retail outlets.

"This is the perfect resource for all who are considering stepfamily living or have already committed. It is not just a book about stepfamilies, but instead a detailed manual on how to create a strong stepfamily unit. The ideas and strategies are clear and compelling. Be prepared to enjoy coming home!"

— Jon Carlson, PsyD, EdD
Author, *Time for a Better Marriage*
Distinguished Professor,
Governors State University

Stepfamilies are different. The "old rules" that govern traditional families don't necessarily apply, and each stepfamily must create its own "new rules" to suit its unique needs. Authors Einstein and Albert bring to this comprehensive guidebook decades of experience as stepfamily therapists, trainers, consultants, acclaimed writers, and stepparents themselves. The result is clear, down-to-earth, expert help for couple relationships and parenting in a stepfamily. Among the many challenges dealt with in this creative book are: overcoming unrealistic expectations, debunking stepfamily myths, decision making, building effective communication, establishing sound discipline, handling stepsibling rivalry, working with non-custodial parents...and more.

More Resources
From Active Parenting

These books are available through your bookstore or from Active Parenting. Check our web site for parenting classes on these subjects in your community, or suggest hosting a class to your child's school, a local religious institution, or adult education provider. Want to teach your own parenting class? Ask about our complete, video-based program kits!

by Michael H. Popkin, PhD
Helps parents of children ages 5 to 12 learn to raise responsible, cooperative children who are prepared to meet the challenges of the teen years and independent living. Also available in Spanish.

by Michael H. Popkin, PhD, Betsy Gard, PhD, and Marilyn Montgomery, PhD
For parents, grandparents, and other caregivers of children ages 1 to 4. Learn a child's stages of development, nonviolent discipline techniques that work, building a bond, and more. Also available in Spanish.

Cooperative Parenting and Divorce

by Susan Boyan, MEd, LMFT, and Ann Marie Termini, EdS, LPC
Ease the transition to a positive new role as "co-parents" with this book that will show how to manage anger, negotiate agreements, and protect children from parental conflict.

by Michael H. Popkin, PhD
For parents of teens and 'tweens. Learn how to communicate effectively with teens, encourage better behavior, teach responsibility, use positive discipline techniques, and more.

by Michael H. Popkin, PhD, Bettie Youngs, PhD, EdD, and Jane Healy, PhD
Parent involvement is key to children's success in school, but it doesn't mean doing their homework for them. This book shows how to support a child by promoting good study habits and working with teachers toward your common goal: a well-educated child.

About the Authors

Michael H. Popkin, PhD, is one of the nation's foremost parenting experts as well as the president and founder of Active Parenting Publishers. He has appeared on CNN, "The Oprah Winfrey Show," and "Montel." A former child and family therapist, Dr. Popkin has written over a dozen books, including his new book, *Taming the Spirited Child* (2007), and several popular video-based discussion programs on parenting. Dr. Popkin received his PhD in Counseling Psychology from Georgia State University. He lives in Atlanta with his wife, Melody, and their two children, Megan and Ben.

Elizabeth Einstein, MA, LMFT, is one of America's leading experts on stepfamily dynamics. She is the author of *Strengthening Your Stepfamily* (2006) and many other books and educational materials. A marriage and family therapist in Ithaca, NY, she presents "Strengthening Stepfamilies" workshops internationally, training professionals and teaching families. She was a founding member of the Stepfamily Association of America, now the National Stepfamily Resource Center. To enlighten and support stepfamilies, Ms. Einstein continues to make media appearances. She grew up in a stepfamily, has two biological sons, and helped raise five stepchildren. Find out more about her work or contact her for training at www.StepfamilyLiving.com.